Amateur Gardening Introduction

Gardening can be as simple or as complicated as you wish to make it. A lot of people are very happy just pottering outdoors, keeping the garden looking tidy and trying something new each year.

In this handbook we've gathered all the important information you need to get the garden looking good through the year. By building on what you already know, you can make your garden the best it can be.

Each month contains timely checklists to jog the memory, plus straightforward advice on essential gardening topics, together with step-by-step instructions to help you carry out tasks with confidence. You'll never be stuck for ideas on what to plant – and be sure to try one of the inspirational weekend projects at the end of each chapter.

There's something for fruit and vegetable lovers, too – we explain how to get the best from your favourite crops and remind you what needs to be sown, planted and harvested each month.

It doesn't matter how long you've been gardening, there's always something new and interesting to learn – just don't forget to enjoy what's in flower in the moment!

Have a great gardening year.

SALLY CHARRETT
EDITOR

Amateur Gardening is the UK's best-selling weekly gardening magazine, and the oldest, launched in 1884. It leads on practical gardening information and its award-winning gardening news pages regularly break major stories. Expert columnists include Bob Flowerdew and Anne Swithinbank from *Gardeners' Question Time*; and former *Gardeners' World* presenters Peter Seabrook and Toby Buckland. *Amateur Gardening* is on sale every Tuesday. For more details, visit:

www.amateurgardening.com

Contents

JANUARY

Even the hardiest of gardeners will spend most of the coldest month of the year indoors – whether that's browsing through the new seed catalogues, fussing over houseplants, or cleaning last year's grime off the pots and seed trays in the shed.

When the weather is clement, there's winter pruning of fruit trees to be done, along with mulching of trees and shrubs, and liming of veg beds if you're planning on growing brassicas. This is also the ideal month to renew blades on mowers and check on the condition of other tools.

Early spring bulbs and occasional bird song remind us that spring is just around the corner.

JANUARY PLANTS 5 OF THE BEST

1 IRIS UNGUICULARIS

Tough winter-flowering iris for full sun. Tidy foliage by pulling out old leaves. **H15in (32cm)**

2 CORNUS SANGUINEA 'MIDWINTER FIRE'

Glowing orange-red stems, good in heavy, wet soils. Cut back hard in late winter. **H5ft (1.5m)**

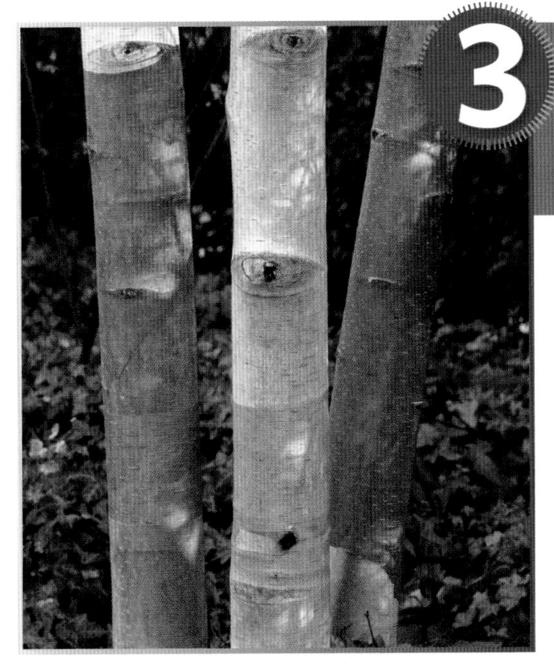

3 BETULA ALBOSINENSIS

A graceful birch with striking pink and copper-coloured bark. **H29-49ft (9-15m)**

4 HAMAMELIS × INTERMEDIA ‘ORANGE PEEL’

Choice witch hazel with scented, light-orange winter blooms; foliage turns buttery yellow and orange in autumn. **H13ft (4m)**

5 ERANTHIS HYEMALIS

Winter aconites form a glowing golden yellow carpet; they look great planted beneath hamamelis. Plant out ‘in the green’. **H3in (8cm)**

OTHERS TO TRY

- *Erica carnea* ‘Myretoun Ruby’
- *Galanthus nivalis*
- *Hamamelis* x *intermedia* ‘Jelena’
- *Jasminum nudiflorum*
- *Narcissus* ‘Rijnveld’s Early Sensation’
- *Narcissus* ‘Ziva’ (indoors)

JANUARY 2014

WEDNESDAY
1

THURSDAY
2

FRIDAY
3

SATURDAY
4

SUNDAY
5

MONDAY
6

TUESDAY
7

WEDNESDAY
8

AT A GLANCE
JOBS TO DO THIS MONTH

GENERAL TASKS

- ☐ Clean, sharpen and oil hand tools.
- ☐ Put the lawn mower in for a service.
- ☐ Spread organic matter over the borders and veg plot on dry days when the soil isn't frozen.
- ☐ Reflect on last year's successes and failures: decide whether there are any parts of the garden you want to change.
- ☐ On dry days, smarten up fences and with paint or preserver.
- ☐ Shred the Christmas tree and add to it to the compost heap.
- ☐ If fish ponds have frozen over; melt a small area of ice by sitting a hot pan on the surface for a few minutes.
- ☐ Provide birds with fresh water and food.
- ☐ Consider buying a water butt.

www.ronseal.co.uk

TREES, SHRUBS CLIMBERS

- ☐ Knock any snow off conifers, evergreens and hedges to avoid branches breaking.
- ☐ Order bare-root roses and plant out when soil conditions allow.

JANUARY 2014

THURSDAY
9

FRIDAY
10

SATURDAY
11

SUNDAY
12

MONDAY
13

TUESDAY
14

WEDNESDAY
15

THURSDAY
16

Galanthus elwesii is an early flowering snowdrop

Your notes

WEATHER:

PLANTS IN BLOOM:

TO DO:

JANUARY 2014

FRIDAY
17

SATURDAY
18

SUNDAY
19

MONDAY
20

TUESDAY
21

WEDNESDAY
22

THURSDAY
23

FRIDAY
24

AT A GLANCE
JOBS TO DO THIS MONTH

FLOWERS

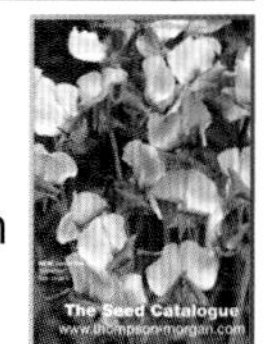

- [ ] Order seed from mail order catalogues.
- [ ] Cut old leaves off hellebores.
- [ ] Order summer-flowering bulbs and perennials for planting in the spring.

PATIOS AND CONTAINERS

- [ ] Deadhead pansies.
- [ ] Water any pots that may have dried out.
- [ ] Scrub slimy patches on the patio with a broom and detergent or pressure washer, if needed.

GREENHOUSE

- [ ] Wash down surfaces, pots and seed trays with hot water and mild detergent, rinse thoroughly.
- [ ] Knock snow off the roof.
- [ ] Sow pelargonium, begonia and lobelia.
- [ ] Check stored dahlias and cannas; remove rotting ones.

WHAT TO PRUNE

- **Wisteria – shorten summer side shoots to two or three buds**
- **Tidy ivies, Virginia creeper and climbing hydrangea to prevent them from working their way into window frames and doors**

JANUARY 2014

SATURDAY
25

SUNDAY
26

MONDAY
27

TUESDAY
28

WEDNESDAY
29

THURSDAY
30

FRIDAY
31

WEATHER:

PLANTS IN BLOOM:

TO DO:

Leave some stems on plants for interest

Get tools into shape

Use the quiet, 'down time' of January to get tools and machinery in order for the season ahead.

Wipe over hand tools with a damp cloth, removing caked-on soil. Let them dry, then rub all wooden parts over with raw linseed oil. It's good to get into the habit of cleaning tools straight after you've used them, to prevent any lurking plant diseases from spreading.

Make sure secateurs and loppers are sharp – there's nothing more frustrating than making the first cut of the year with a blunt blade. Use a sharpening block (whetstone) or metal file. Other cutting edges such as spades, knives and hoes can also be sharpened this way.

If you're in need of new tools, try to buy good quality ones that will last, rather than cheaper alternatives, and handle a tool before you buy it to make sure it's comfortable to hold. Keep an eye out in charity shops and car boot sales for good second-hand tools. Stainless steel is the best material and will last a lifetime.

Wash and check over gardening gloves for tears or broken seams; replace if necessary.

Lastly, if the blades on your mower are blunt (whether petrol or electric) have them sharpened and balanced by a local expert.

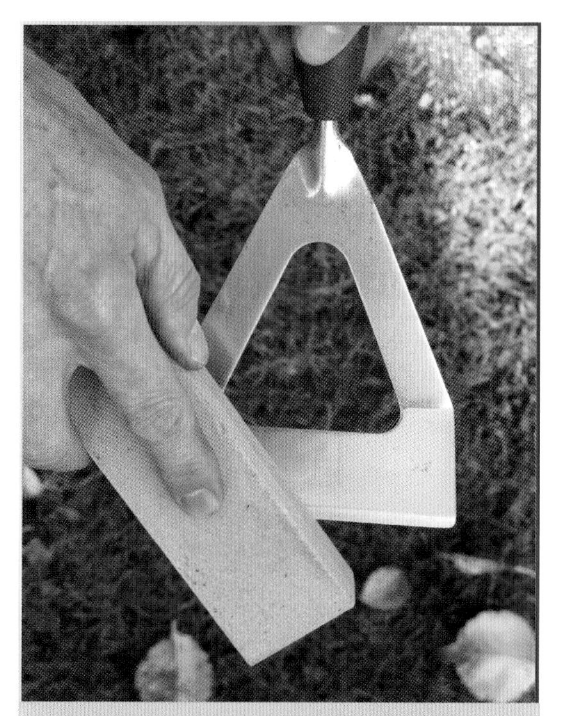

Cutting edges can be sharpened with a metal file or a sharpening block

Step by step Cleaning and sharpening secateurs

1 Oil all moving parts. Spray metal parts with a lubricating oil such as WD40 to loosen caked-on grime and hardened sap from the blades.

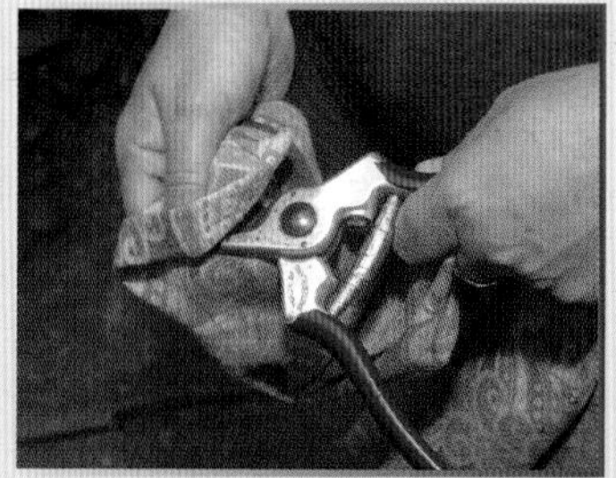

2 Use wire wool or a cloth to rub down all metal parts – this will remove sap stains and other grime loosened by the oil.

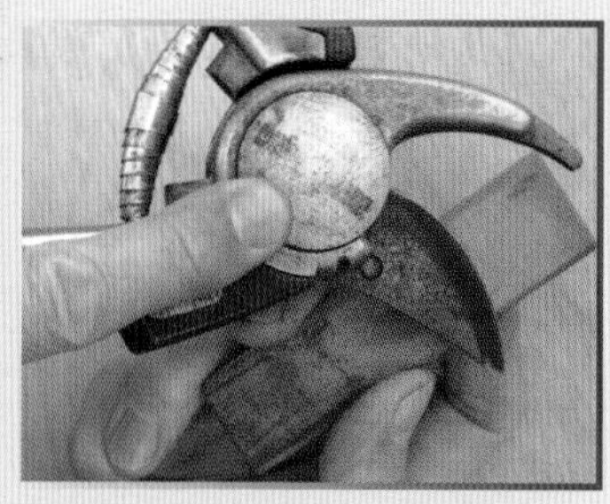

3 To sharpen blade, run it across a whetstone several times in a sweeping motion, pushing forward across the stone.

WOODEN HANDLES

- **Always allow wooden parts to dry out before putting them away, standing them upright to receive good sunlight.**
- **Before putting hand tools away for winter, rub all wooden parts down with raw linseed oil. This prevents drying out and splintering and gives the wood a soft feel.**

MOWER MAINTENENCE

ELECTRIC

Never have mowers connected to the mains when working on them. Brush down the blades after each use and oil all working parts (this applies to petrol mowers, too).

PETROL

Always disconnect the spark plug lead when the mower is not in use and run down the fuel towards the end of the season, before storing over winter. Drain and replace oil. Remove and check air filter; replace if dirty.

SUNDRIES

- DO AN INVENTORY

Check whether you're in need of any sundries: garden centres will be well-stocked now ahead of the mad rush in spring.

- [ ] **Plastic seed trays & pots**
- [ ] **Garden twine**
- [ ] **Labels**
- [ ] **Canes**
- [ ] **Watering can with a fine rose**
- [ ] **Garden fork and spade**
- [ ] **Hand trowel and fork**
- [ ] **Seed compost**
- [ ] **Multi-purpose compost**
- [ ] **Good pair of secateurs**
- [ ] **General-purpose fertiliser**
- [ ] **Loppers**

Consider investing in a heated propagator to help your early seedlings along. (inset picture, above) Bottle-top waterers are a brilliant way to water new seedlings

Good time to order seeds

It's still a good few weeks before you can properly get out into the garden, so enjoy the pause in the gardening calendar, and relax with a stack of seed catalogues indoors, instead.

Fantasising about how you'd like the garden to look this year and making 'wish-lists' is the perfect antidote to grey, wintry days. Imagine there's no spending limit and write as long a list as you dare, then whittle it down to something more realistic. This is a good way of discovering what you really want to do with your plot. Explore more unusual catalogues, too, as well the reliable old favourites.

It's still too early to sow most seeds or plant out, but order now while stock levels are high to get the best choices. Most companies won't send out plug plants until the weather warms up, but at least you've got your order in.

Sort through old seed packets to see what you've got before placing any new orders

6 of the best seed catalogues

■ Thompson and Morgan
Large international company. Reliable seeds, comprehensive information on the website. Always lots of tempting goodies.
Tel 0844 248 5383
www.thompson-morgan.com

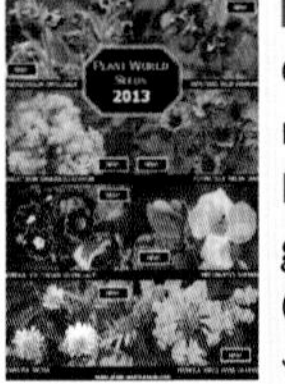

■ Plant World Seeds
Offers an unusual, exotic and exciting range of flowers and vegetable seed. Excellent reputation, many top gardeners rave about this company.
01803 872939
www.plant-world-seeds.com

■ Seeds of Italy
Good-looking, heirloom Italian vegetable varieties selected for their flavour. A must for keen veg growers and cooks alike.
0208 427 5020
www.seedsofitaly.com

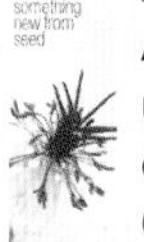

■ Chiltern Seeds
Always a pleasure to leaf through – has many unusual varieties for sale and the written descriptions of plants are a joy to read.
01491 824675
www.chilternseeds.co.uk

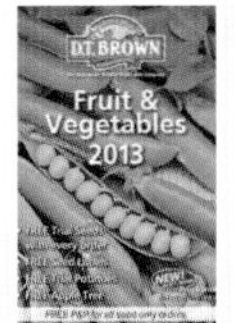

■ DT Brown
Somewhere between a family run business and large corporate company. Good range of onions, potatoes and sweet peas.
0845 3710532
www.dtbrownseeds.co.uk

■ Mr Fothergills
Another long-established seed company that is reliably good. Great germination, good prices, free mail order.
0845 3710518
www.mr-fothergills.co.uk

MAKING SENSE OF SEED CATALOGUES

Below is a general guide of when to sow or grow the seeds, bulbs or plants you're likely to find in catalogues. Always follow specific advice on the back of packets:

- **Hardy annuals:** Sow outdoors in autumn or March/April.
- **Half-hardy annuals:** Begonias, lobelia and pelargonium can be sown undercover as early as January; others, such as cosmos and petunia are sown later in spring; plant out when all threat of frost has passed.

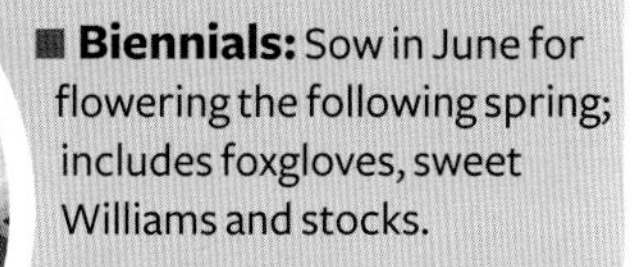

- **Biennials:** Sow in June for flowering the following spring; includes foxgloves, sweet Williams and stocks.
- **Plug plants:** Companies will start despatching from March, but will hold plugs back in very cold weather. Pot up immediately on receipt.
- **Spring bulbs:** Usually despatched from late summer. Plant out in autumn.
- **Summer bulbs:** Plant outdoors in spring when the soil is warming up.
- **Dahlia tubers:** Pot them up into compost March/April, keep somewhere frost-free and plant out when all threat of frost has passed.
- **Autumn bulbs:** For the best displays, plant out autumn and winter-flowering bulbs in spring.
- **Perennials from seed:** Sow in autumn for the best results; plants will have had time to bulk up before planting out in the spring.
- **Young pot-grown perennials:** Autumn is the ideal time to plant out, but spring is ok, too.

While the garden is in its dormant state, step outside and assess what's working and what's not. Is there room to expand a border or make the shape of the lawn more interesting? Are any plants not earning their keep?

Designer tricks of the trade

• INTEREST
Create a sense of adventure by including several focal points to draw the visitor in. This could be a large eye-catching urn, a tinkling water feature, or a statue in the borders.

• ADD HEIGHT
A garden is much more interesting if there is a mixture of plant heights, from columnar trees to groundcover. Also consider building a couple of raised beds or a raised seating area.

• HIDE EYESORES
Think about planting evergreen or annual climbers to hide unsightly walls and fences.

• UNITY
This means making sure everything in the garden 'hangs together' – romantic cottage garden plants are going to look odd against the harsh brick of a modern house, for instance.

• CONTRAST
Within the boundaries of unity, there should be contrast, particularly in the borders. This could be contrasting flower colours or contrast in leaf shape, colour and texture.

Grow your own rhubarb

Rhubarb is very easy to grow and suffers few pest and disease problems. It's a great crop for gardeners in cold parts of the country, as it's fully hardy; it actually tastes better in cooler conditions.

The natural time to harvest rhubarb is spring, but it's worth forcing it in January or February to get an early crop of beautifully pink, sweet stems at a time when not much other fruit is around.

The best time to plant new rhubarb plants (one-year-old crowns) is late autumn to early winter, but you can plant in the spring, too. Prepare the soil thoroughly in advance: rhubarb develops a deep root system and grows best in a fertile, partially shaded, free-draining soil. If the soil is too wet, crowns will be vulnerable to crown rot. Add as much organic matter such as well-rotted manure or garden compost as you can. Don't harvest stems in the first year as this will affect vigour.

Plants can get big over time (3ft by 4ft), so bear this in mind when you are choosing your site.

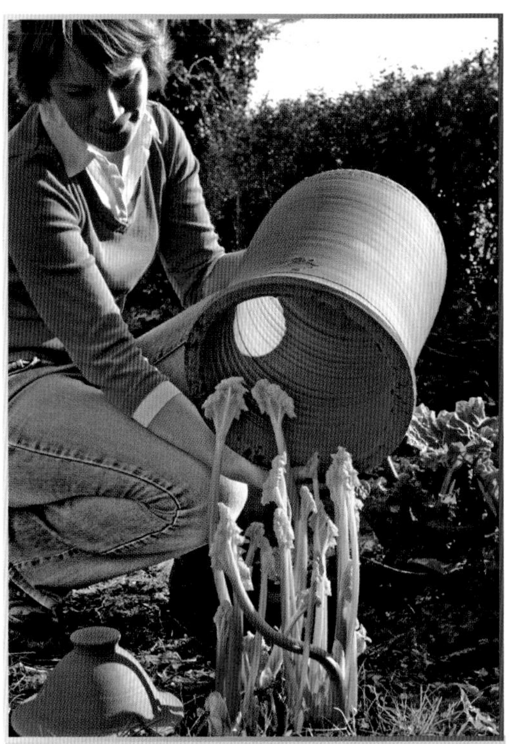

FORCING STEMS

In January and February, force early stems by covering the crown with an upturned bin or terracotta rhubarb forcer (above). Mulch with manure first to create extra warmth and speed up the process. Check after 4-5 weeks, and pick the blanched, pink stems.

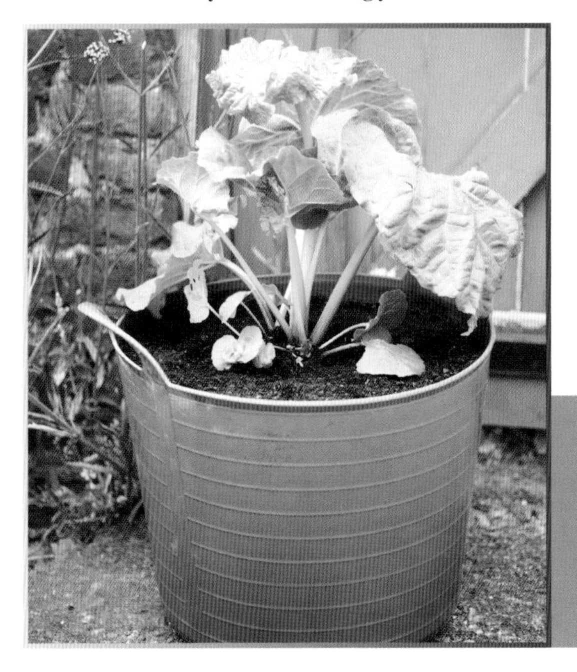

IN CONTAINERS

You can grow rhubarb in a container, but it will need to be at least 20in (50cm) deep and wide. Drill holes in the bottom of the tub if it doesn't have drainage holes. Fill with a soil-based compost like John Innes No3 and add in extra organic matter.

THE ESSENTIALS

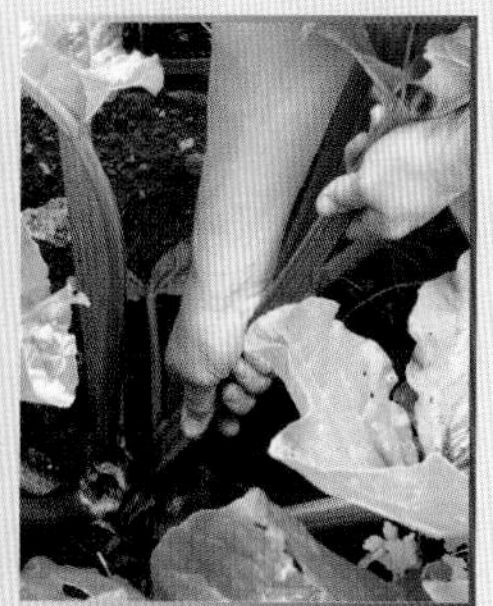

1 PLANTING

In late autumn/early winter, set the crowns/ plants in the soil so the buds just show at the surface. Water in really well and leave to settle for the first year before harvesting any stems.

2 PICKING

When harvesting rhubarb, it's important to pull stems off plants rather than cutting them as cutting can let in infection. Only eat the stems – the leaves are poisonous.

3 DIVIDING

Lift and divide plants every 3-5 years. Chop the plant into sections with a fork or spade, ensuring each section has a bud or young shoot that will form next year's shoots.

4 ROUTINE CARE

Cut off flowers if they develop. Feed with a balanced fertiliser after picking. Water in dry spells and mulch in the autumn. If your plant has lots of skinny stems it needs dividing or feeding.

VARIETIES TO TRY

- **'Champagne'** – good for forcing
- **'Glaskin's Perpetual'** – crops over a long period
- **'Timperley Early'** – very early and one of the best for forcing
- **'Victoria'** – late type with good yields

January

THE EDIBLE GARDEN - OTHER JOBS TO DO THIS MONTH

PLANT OUT

- Still okay to plant out garlic
- Plant bare-root fruit trees when the weather is clement

HARVEST

- Sprouting broccoli, kale, celeriac and perpetual spinach

PRUNE

- Standard apple and pear trees, blackberries, currants and gooseberries

GENERAL TASKS

- **Add manure** to the veg plot if not done before now
- **Cover the ground** with polythene to warm the soil for early sowing or planting
- **Order seed potatoes** and onion sets
- **Apply organic** fertiliser such as blood, fish and bone to the soil
- **Mulch newly** planted fruit trees
- **Feed fruit plants** with an organic fertiliser like blood, fish and bone

January project

Plan a cut flower garden

BY DEDICATING a part of the garden to growing cut flowers, you can really focus on releasing your inner florist. Raised beds are ideal as they provide excellent drainage – you could even make an attractive feature of them by laying them out in a formal parterre-style, with pathways in between for easy access.

Grow the flowers in rows to make hoeing easier and to give each plant a little more room than it might get in a mixed bed.

To keep costs down, grow everything from seed – hardy and half-hardy annuals.

Sit down with a stack of seed catalogues and make lists of what to grow. Split your flower choices into three sections: 'wow factor' flowers (the central blooms), 'satellite' flowers (softer-looking blooms to go around the wow-factor ones), and a range of really reliable green plants to provide a framework.

By June you'll be picking the first gorgeous blooms of your labours – and you should have an unending supply of material right up until the first frosts.

Let some of the plants go to seed – you can save money by collecting your own seed.

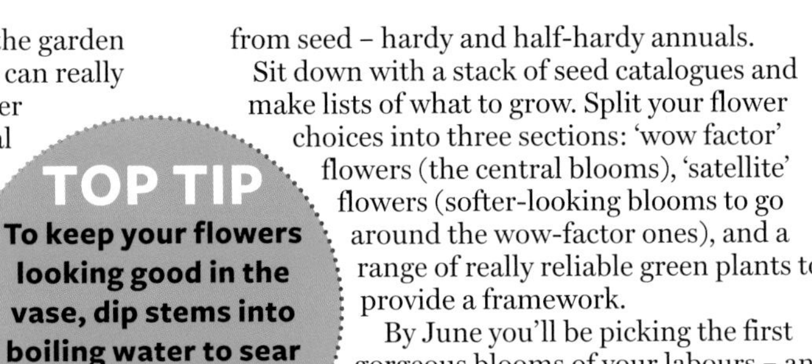

TOP TIP

To keep your flowers looking good in the vase, dip stems into boiling water to sear for a few minutes before arranging

Step by step Getting started

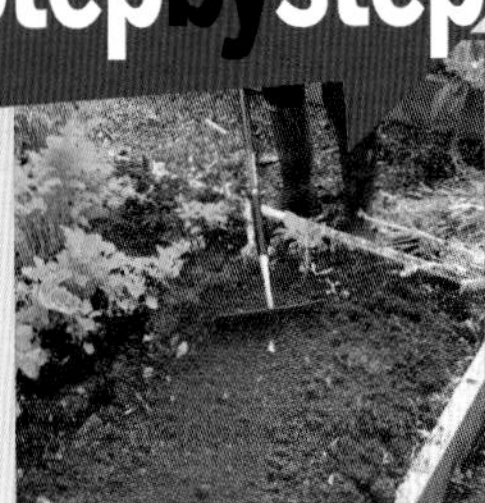

1 Choose a sunny location – either clear a piece of ground or use an area of an existing veg plot. Add garden compost to the soil if needed and mix in grit if you have heavy clay soil. Rake into a fine tilth.

2 Sow half-hardy annuals in trays and pots indoors from around February; some can be sown directly into the soil later on – check packets for instructions. Plant out in rows from early May and label clearly.

3 From April onwards sow hardy annuals outside directly into the soil. Continue to sow hardy annuals until September to keep your supplies going. Spread seeds out as you sow, to save thinning out later.

4 Water well for the first few weeks, weed between rows regularly, and apply your chosen slug controls. Taller, flimsy flowers such as some rudbeckias, nicotiana, scabious and zinnias will need staking.

BEST BLOOMS TO GROW
TO GET THE FLORIST'S LOOK!

WOW FACTOR BLOOMS

Place these at the centre of bouquets as a starting point

- **Nicotiana 'Perfume Deep Purple'** – half hardy annual. An intoxicating dark shade, eye catching. Soft perfume in evening. Start indoors. Stake.
- **Zinnia 'Starlight Rose' and 'Purple Prince'** – half hardy annuals. Bright colours with useful straight stems. Sow undercover March-May, or sow direct after last frost.
- **Rudbeckia 'Marakesh Market'** – half hardy annual (pictured). Dramatic flowers in a range of terracottas, golds and burnished orange. Upright stems with velvety leaves.
- **Cosmos bipinnatus 'Psyche White'** – a striking cut flower with large, wavy pure-white blooms. Half-hardy annual.

SATELLITE FLOWERS

Work these 'filler' blooms around the central wow factor ones

- **Salvia farinacea 'Victoria'** (half-hardy) and *Salvia viridis* 'Blue' (hardy). Blues and mauves.
- **Calendula 'Porcupine' (marigolds)** – sow direct. Frilly orange blooms for months.
- **Scabious atropurpurea 'Black Knight'** (pictured). Hardy annual. Velvet crimson flowers with long stems. Insects adore them. Stake.

- **Nasturtium 'Saucy Rascal'** – sow direct. Bright pastel flowers with marbled foliage.
- **Nigella 'Double White'** – hardy annual (pictured). Useful as cut flower or as dried seed heads. There is a blue variety, too.

- **Californian poppy** – hardy annual. Eye catching oranges and yellows.
- **Browallia 'Blue Lady'** – Half hardy annual, start indoors. Pretty dainty blue flowers.

GREEN FOILS

Use these plants to provide a framework for bouquets

- **Ammi majus 'Bishop's Flower'** – Hardy annual. Lacy cow-parsley like flowers which add a country feel to arrangements.
- **Cerinthe major 'Purpurascens'** – hardy annual. Silvery green leaves, deep-purple bell-shaped flowers, which flower from spring. Looks good with almost anything.
- **Smyrnium perfoliatum** – curious spring plant with rounded leaves that encircle the stems. Brilliant with tulips and wallflowers.
- **Euphorbia oblongata** – acid-green flowers, fantastic for giving body to arrangements (pictured). Contrasts well with bright flowers.
- **Ornamental kale 'Peacock Rouge'** – wonderful, frilly purple-blue foliage, use the outside leaves to edge bouquets, or cut whole stems. Sow direct or in pots undercover.

FEBRUARY

It may still be nasty outdoors, but a whole host of plants – from wisteria to ornamental grasses – need pruning this month, so wrap up warm and get busy on dry days.

Shops will have seed potatoes in stock, and these can be set out in seed trays to 'chit'. You can also sow veg seeds of parsnips, tomatoes, cucumbers and peppers, as well as half-hardy annuals indoors for the flower garden; fussy seeds such as petunias, impatiens and begonias prefer a heated propagator.

If the weather's been mild you may need to give the lawn its first cut; make sure the blades are set high and add the cuttings to the compost heap.

FEBRUARY PLANTS 5 OF THE BEST

1 CROCUS TOMMASINIANUS

Late winter bulb with eye-catching lilac blooms. Self-seeds readily – one of the easiest to naturalise. **H4in (10cm)**

2 EUONYMUS FORTUNEI 'EMERALD AND GOLD'

Versatile evergreen shrub, good for adding structure to the garden. Golden variegated foliage brightens up the borders. **H2ft (60cm)**

3 CAMELLIA X WILLIAMSII 'ANTICIPATION'

Upright evergreen shrub. One of the toughest and easiest camellias to grow. Peony-like flowers Feb/Mar. **H9ft (3m)**

4 NARCISSUS 'FEBRUARY GOLD'

Classic miniature variety with swept-back petals. Plant lots together in large drifts for the best effect. Flowers Feb/Mar. **H1ft (30cm)**

5 GALANTHUS 'MAGNET'

One of the best snowdrops. Large blooms on long stalks. Honey-like scent in the sunshine. Good for early pollinators. **H4in (10cm)**

OTHERS TO TRY

- *Acacia dealbata*
- *Camellia* 'Takanini'
- *Cornus officinalis*
- *Crocus* 'Zwanenburg Bronze'
- *Daphne odora* 'Aureomarginata'
- *Forsythia* 'Lynwood Variety'
- *Helleborus foetidus*
- *Helleborus x hybridus*
- *Iris reticulata*
- *Prunus mume* 'Beni-chidori'

FEBRUARY 2014

SATURDAY
1

SUNDAY
2

MONDAY
3

TUESDAY
4

WEDNESDAY
5

THURSDAY
6

FRIDAY
7

SATURDAY
8

AT A GLANCE
JOBS TO DO THIS MONTH

GENERAL TASKS

- ☐ Order plug plants.
- ☐ Finish off winter digging/manuring.
- ☐ Create new beds and borders to make way for any new design plans.
- ☐ Provide food for birds – it's a very hungry month for wildlife.

LAWNS

- ☐ Mow lawn if mild and dry, keeping blades high, and prepare ground for a new lawn if required.

TREES, SHRUBS AND CLIMBERS

- ☐ Plant bare-root trees and shrubs and move deciduous woody plants.
- ☐ Take hardwood cuttings (can be taken anytime between mid autumn and late winter).
- ☐ Cut back dogwood hard, for colourful stems next winter (pictured below).

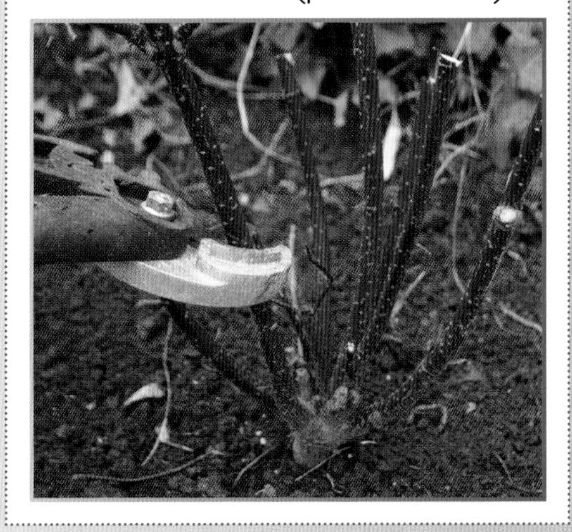

FEBRUARY 2014

SUNDAY
9

MONDAY
10

TUESDAY
11

WEDNESDAY
12

THURSDAY
13

FRIDAY
14

SATURDAY
15

SUNDAY
16

February is a hungry month for birds

Your notes

WEATHER:

PLANTS IN BLOOM:

TO DO:

FEBRUARY 2014

MONDAY
17

TUESDAY
18

WEDNESDAY
19

THURSDAY
20

FRIDAY
21

SATURDAY
22

SUNDAY
23

MONDAY
24

AT A GLANCE
JOBS TO DO THIS MONTH

FLOWERS

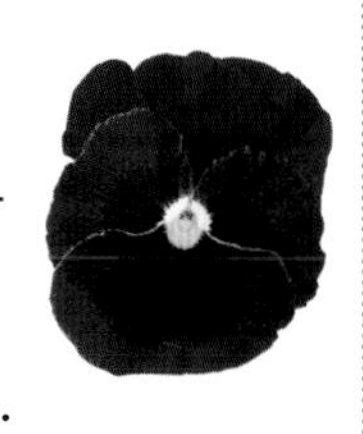

- ☐ Plant out pot-grown spring bulbs and polyanthus for instant colour (harden off first).
- ☐ Tidy and deadhead winter pansies.
- ☐ Start off dahlia tubers in trays or pots.
- ☐ Add some winter colour to borders.
- ☐ Divide snowdrops after flowering.
- ☐ Order summer bulbs for spring planting.

IN THE GREENHOUSE

- ☐ Sow sweet peas, lobelia, begonias impatiens and pelargonium.

CONTAINERS AND PATIOS

- ☐ Water and top-dress long-term permanent pots.
- ☐ Treat yourself to a winter-flowering scented shrub in a pot like *Sarcococca confusa* (plant out into the garden after a couple of years).

WHAT TO PRUNE

- **Winter jasmine**
- **Buddleja davidii**
- **Deciduous ceanothus**
- **Hardy fuchsias**
- **Late-flowering clematis**
- **Ornamental grasses**
- **Leycesteria**
- **Trim winter heathers as flowers fade**
- **Last chance to prune wisteria**

FEBRUARY 2014

TUESDAY
25

WEDNESDAY
26

THURSDAY
27

FRIDAY
28

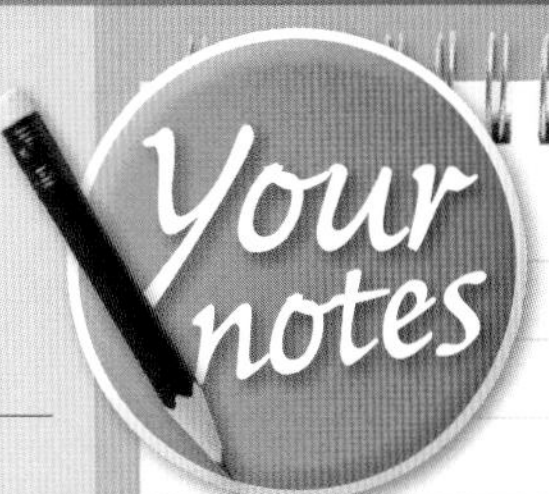

WEATHER:

PLANTS IN BLOOM:

TO DO:

Plant out primoses to brighten up the borders

Prune and care for clematis

The question of how and when to prune clematis often leaves gardeners wringing their hands and scratching their heads.

An easy-to-remember rule of thumb is: "if it flowers before June, don't prune". In other words, any clematis that flowers before Midsummer's Day doesn't require regular pruning – just a tidy up. These early types (also known as Group I clematis) include: winter-flowering *C. cirrhosa*, and spring-flowering *C. armandii, C. alpina, C. macropetala* and *C. montana*.

The later-flowering types however, must be pruned now, before active growth begins. These include large-flowered clematis (which bloom from early summer, often with a second flush of flowers in September) and late-summer varieties. The latter are the simplest to prune – cut all shoots down to a strong pair of leaf buds 6-12in (15-30cm) from the ground. Large-flowered early summer varieties are more fiddly: remove about a quarter of the top growth in February, cutting each stem back to the nearest pair of healthy leaf buds. These types also enjoy being cut back halfway after their first flush of flowers.

With all clematis, ensure plants are kept healthy by removing any dead, diseased or dying stems.

Key to pruning

Each clematis belongs to a particular pruning group; the key to pruning your clematis is knowing what type you have. It's a good idea to keep the labels of any you buy, so that you can check the specific pruning requirements.

Step by step How to prune

GROUP II Light-prune

- 'Nelly Moser'
- 'Arctic Queen'
- 'Rebecca'
- 'Diana's Delight'
- 'Crystal Fountain'

Remove a quarter of the top growth, cutting each stem back to the nearest pair of healthy leaf buds

GROUP III Hard-prune

- 'Etoile Violette'
- 'Vienetta'
- *C.florida*
- *C.viticella*
- 'Star of India'
- 'Hagley Hybrid'

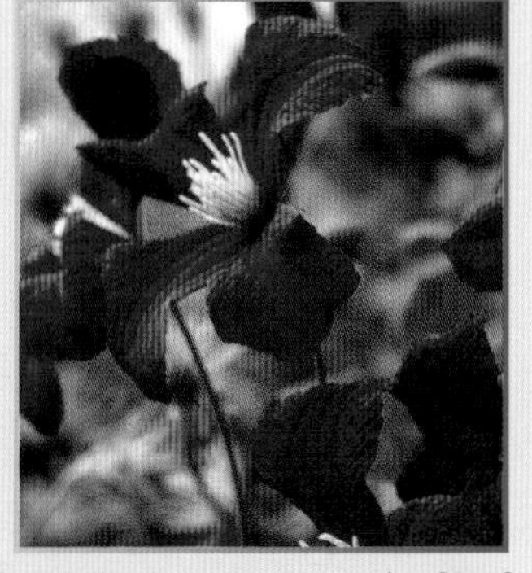

Cut all shoots back hard, down to a strong pair of leaf buds 6-12in (15-30cm) from the ground

GROWING CLEMATIS IN POTS

With thanks to Raymond Evison Clematis

Use a moisture-retentive compost, such as loam-based John Innes No3, adding in handfuls of grit. Plant in containers that are at least 18in (45cm) deep and wide. Place in cane supports before planting; tie in the growth. Keep the container moist and add a mulch over roots.

 **Varieties to try:**

'Picardy'
'Ooh La La'
'Rouge Cardinal'

CLEMATIS CARE THROUGH THE YEAR

- **Late winter –** prune Group II and III
- **Spring –** tidy up Group I.
- **April –** good time to plant clematis; plant evergreen species with the crown at soil level, others 2in (5cm) deeper. Make sure the planting hole is twice the width of the rootball and add in garden compost or well-rotted manure.
- **Any newly planted** clematis should be cut back to 6in-12in (15-30cm) from ground level, cutting just above a bud.
- **Summer –** Water thoroughly during hot, dry spells and place pebbles or stones at the base to keep roots cool.
- **April-Sep –** clematis are hungry plants: give them a liquid potash feed monthly to promote flower bud formation.

3 clematis problems resolved

Q Some of the shoots are wilting at the tips and dying back. What has caused this?

A There are a number of possibilities. If your plant is a large-flowered hybrid, then it may have the fungal disease clematis wilt. Cut out all affected shoots back to healthy growth and destroy infected parts. Plants in pots may also be susceptible to vine weevil grubs or waterlogged roots.

Q Why won't my clematis flower?

A There are several reasons why this could be. The most likely is not enough sunshine getting to the top of plants. Clematis need their roots kept cool and shaded, but flowering will be impaired if the top of the plant is kept in deep shade. It may also be in need of a feed – apply sulphate of potash in later winter/early spring.

Q My clematis is all woody at the base and only flowers at the top.

A It's likely that you aren't regularly pruning it. The good news is that clematis from all three groups can be renovated by hard pruning almost back to the base (1-3ft/30-90cm). The best time to do this is spring; apply a general fertiliser, mulch and water in dry periods. Leave it at least three years before hard pruning again.

Viticella clematis give a much needed shot of colour in late summer, and are easy to prune

Plant bare-root trees & shrubs

Bare-root woody plants such as trees, hedging, fruit and roses can be planted anytime between November and March, provided the soil isn't frozen or waterlogged. However, February is an ideal time as it won't be long before the soil begins to warm up and new roots will soon romp away. Whatever time you choose, the planting method is generally the same for all bare-root plants, and as long as you stick to a few basic rules, you won't go far wrong.

Bare-roots are supplied without pots or soil. While their pot-grown counterparts can be bought at any time of year, bare-roots must be planted in the garden during their dormant, leafless state. They aren't much to look at on delivery – often just a bundle of 'sticks' with roots attached – but don't let that disappoint. The main advantage of bare-roots over pot-grown plants is cost – they're cheaper for nurserymen to produce, so the retail price is kept down, and also you get a lot more plant for your money, as their roots have been grown in open soil and not confined in a pot.

For the widest choice, seek a specialist mail order/ online retailer – garden centres do stock bare-roots but these are often only fruit trees.

Step by step: How to plant bare-roots

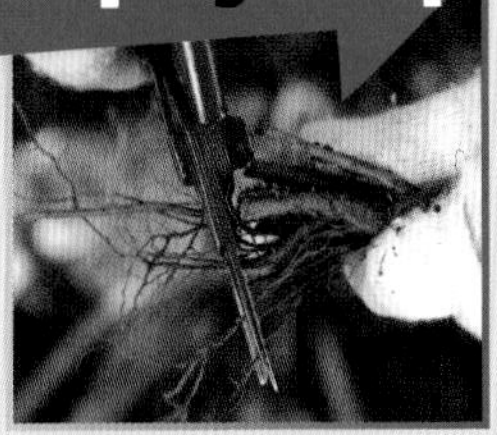

1 Trim off any damaged roots and cut back over-long roots. Improve the planting site by adding garden compost or well-rotted manure.

2 Dig a hole just deep enough to be able to spread the roots out in the bottom, and up to three times the diameter of the root system.

3 Set your plant at the same depth as the soil mark at the base of the stem. Planting too deep is a common cause of tree death.

4 Fill the hole in stages, wiggling the plant as you go, to knock out any air gaps. Water thoroughly and apply a mulch.

THE DOS

■ Prepare the soil well before planting, digging in organic matter and slow-release bonemeal. If you just add a handful of fertiliser to the hole, it's likely that the roots won't venture out to the surrounding soil.

■ Before planting, soak plant roots in a bucket of water, so that they are are moist before planting. If you can't find a bucket big enough, just ensure you give plants a good watering once they're in the soil.

■ Always plant trees and shrubs to the 'high-tide' mark left from the soil at the nursery.

■ Wiggle plants around after you have backfilled the planting hole, to make sure there are no air pockets; top up the soil level if necessary.

■ Water plants in well, even if rain is forecast.

■ Support trees with stakes and ties (above).

THE DON'TS

■ Don't plant when the soil is waterlogged or frozen to give plants the best start.

■ Don't leave newly bought plants lying around to dry out; if planting is delayed, plants can be temporarily heeled into a trench (above) until you are ready to plant.

■ Don't bend roots to fit the planting hole – ensure the hole is big enough in the first place.

■ Don't forget to regularly water during the first year of planting. This is crucial for helping plants to establish.

ROSES

Gardeners are always debating whether roses should be planted with the scion (the graft-joint between roots and stem) above or below soil level. The latest advice from the RHS is to plant with the union just above the surface.

FRUIT

If you want to train a fruit tree into a fan, espalier or cordon, a bare-root tree is usually the best and cheapest way to start. Plum trees are particularly good bare-root options in winter, as container-grown plums can be difficult to establish during the cold season.

Sow great sweet peas

Growers of sweet peas tend to fall into one of two camps. The vast majority sow their seed around late February/early March for mid-summer flowers; others will sow in earnest during autumn, overwintering the young plants to encourage them to flower a month or so earlier than the spring-sown types.

Both camps are absolutely fine. But if you're time-pressed or are new to sowing sweet peas, February is an excellent time to sow.

There's no need to soak or rub the seed coat – viable seeds will germinate usually within 15 days. Sweet peas will need a bit of warmth to germinate – a sunny windowsill is ideal – but once the seedlings come through, keep them cool and moist, ideally at a temperature of 5°c (41°F).

Once the seedlings have three pairs of true leaves pinch out the tops to encourage bushier plants. After the roots have filled their pots, move them outside to harden them off before planting them into fertile, deeply dug soil, spacing them 6in (15cm) apart.

For the following five or six weeks, try to water them in the morning or evening, rather than at midday. Don't feed with extra nitrogen – the pea and bean family resents it. Give a weekly feed of high-potash tomato fertiliser once flowering starts.

Did you know?

Sweet pea seeds will come true to type. The flowers self-pollinate themselves whilst in tight bud, so insects are unable to cross-pollinate. Let plants set seed in August and collect them once they are dry and brown.

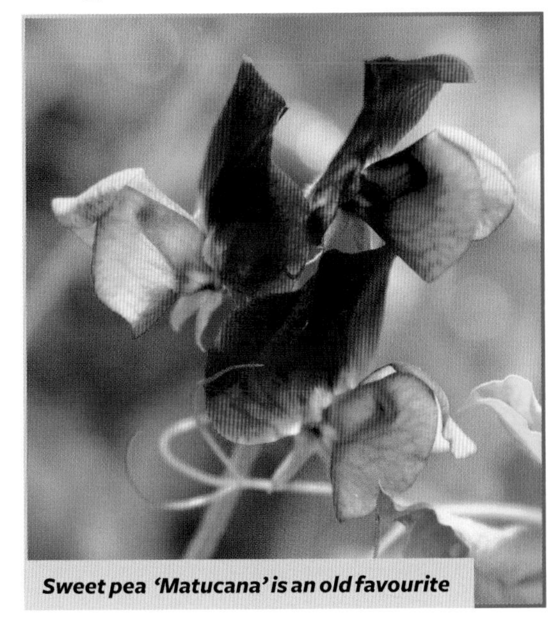

Sweet pea 'Matucana' is an old favourite

Step by step: How to sow

1 Three-quarters fill deep pots such as grow tubes or root trainers with seed compost. Water well then top up with dry compost.

2 Sow the seeds, 1in deep. Label clearly. For good germination rates, place somewhere warm – but not in a heated propagator.

3 Cover the pots with a sheet of newspaper. Don't water again until germination occurs – usually within 15 days.

AS CUT FLOWERS

Sweet peas look stunning in simple vases – and the more you pick them, the more the flowers will keep coming. There's no special technique to cutting them, but early morning is best, and put them straight into water. They combine well with lots of other flowers:

- ***Alchemilla mollis***
- ***Clary sage***
- ***Cornflowers***
- ***Scabious***
- ***Ammi majus***
- ***Calendula 'Indian Prince'***
- ***Dill flowers***

Sweet peas need to climb up supports; try bamboo canes or a wicker obelisk

VARIETIES TO TRY

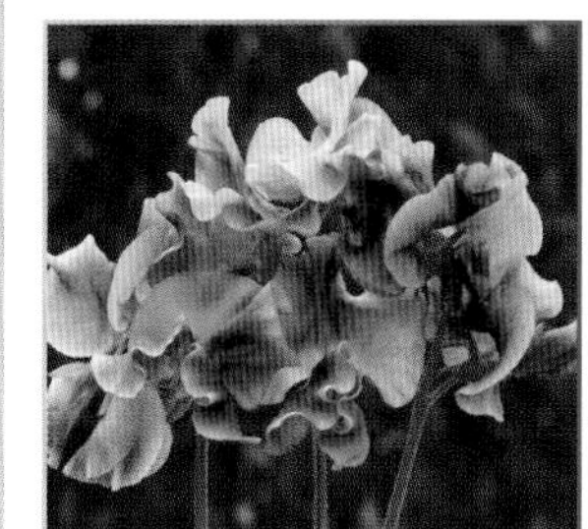

'Our Harry': Gorgeous lavender-blue sweet pea with wavy petals and fragrance. An excellent cut flower.

'Albutt Blue': Lovely white blooms with a dainty purplish blue picoteed edge. Fabuous scent.

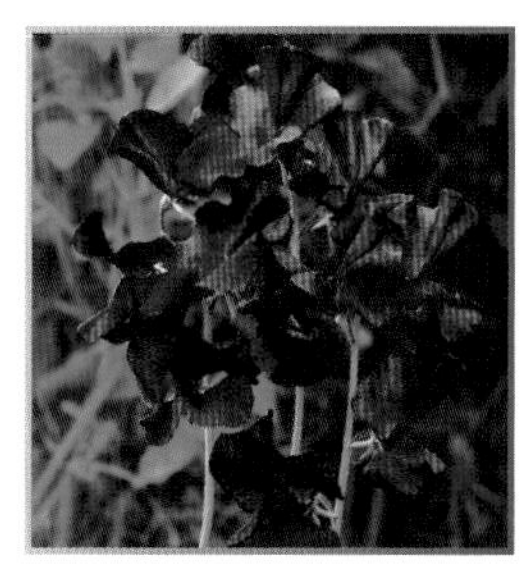

'Windsor': A deep-maroon red that comes to life when the sun shines; the only red sweet pea with a good scent.

'Pulsar' (syn 'Lilac Ripple): The best of the flaked two-tone sweet peas. This lilac and white has a strong scent. Good for garden or vase.

'Gwendoline': Large and dramatic with wavy cerise-pink blooms on a white ground. Strong stems and a heady perfume. Good for the garden or cutting.

With thanks to: www.simplyseedsandplants.co.uk

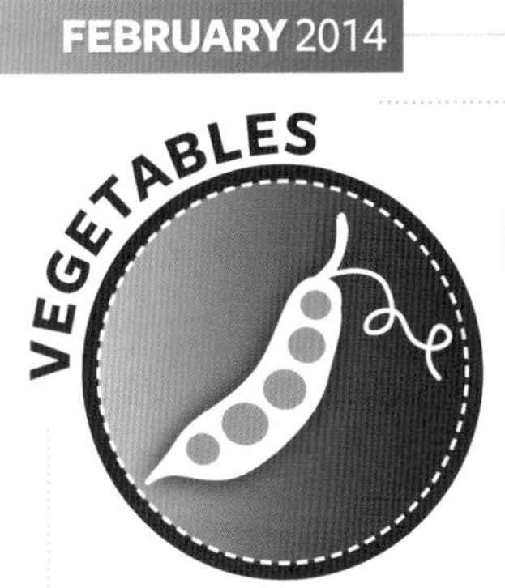

Chit seed potatoes

By placing seed potatoes in a cool, light place such as a windowsill, you'll encourage them to sprout strong greenish-purple shoots (not the pale brittle ones you would get if they were in the dark). This process is called chitting and gardeners are usually advised to do this six weeks before planting tubers out. Commercial growers don't normally bother with chitting and a lot of experts agree that it's unnecessary and doesn't make any difference to the harvest time – but other growers swear by it.

Whichever camp you're in, it's worth chitting early potatoes, as the idea is to get these types to mature as quickly as possible. You can start chitting early potatoes from late January in milder parts for really early crops of new potatoes. Beware that frost will damage plants so keep containers in a greenhouse and place fleece over outdoor crops until the weather starts to warm up.

Most companies start to sell seed potatoes early in the new year, so place your order in good time to get the widest choice.

TOP TIP

Avoid planting in soil where potatoes have grown for two years in succession to reduce the risk of disease

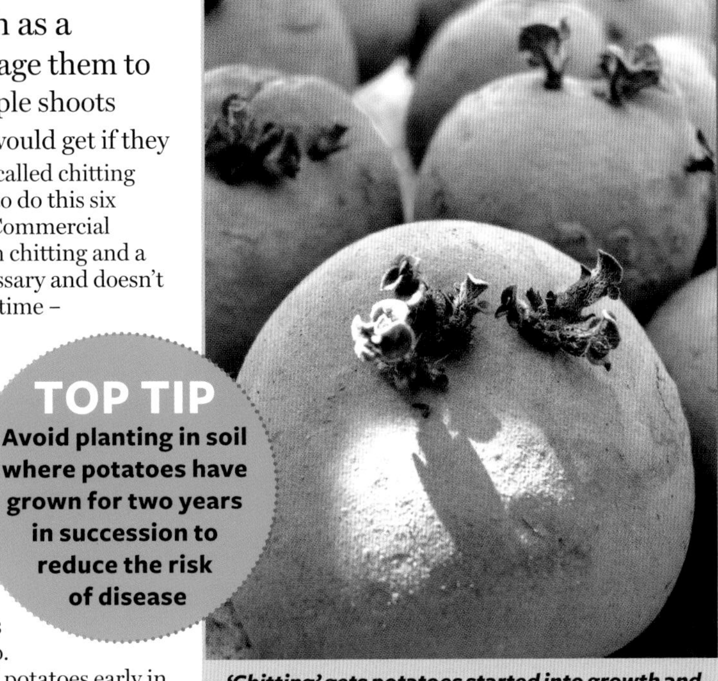

'Chitting' gets potatoes started into growth and is a good way to check that tubers are healthy

PLANTING GUIDE

Potatoes are grouped according to the length of time to maturity and time of harvest:

- **Earlies –** plant March; harvest late May
- **Second earlies –** plant mid-March/ early April ; harvest late July/early Aug
- **Main crop –** plant late March/early April; lift from July to October
- **Salad** (those with waxy flesh – there are varieties in every group)

VARIETIES TO TRY

- **'Epicure'** 1st early (fluffy flesh)
- **'International Kidney'** (Jersey Royals) – second early
- **'Ratte' –** maincrop salad (firm flesh)
- **'Cara' –** maincrop with a fluffy flesh
- **'Charlotte' 2nd early –** very flexible, can used in salads, made into chips, baked or boiled

Grow potatoes

IN THE GROUND

SITE & SOIL

Potatoes need deep fertile soil that is on the acidic side – add garden compost or well-rotted manure to soil in autumn. The site should be sunny with the soil temperature at least 6°C (43°F).

PLANT OUT

Set earlies 6in(15cm) deep and 12in (30cm) apart in rows 24in (60cm) apart. Set second earlies and maincrops at the same depth but with a bit more room between tubers and rows. Earth up when stems are 4in (10cm) high. Repeat a couple more times as they grow.

HARVEST

After flowering, check early varieties – scrape away soil/compost to see if tubers have formed. When you find them, lift a few plants with a fork, but give the rest 2-3 more weeks. Lift second earlies and maincrops when the tops start to die down.

IN CONTAINERS

The easiest way to grow potatoes is in old compost bags or containers – although you won't achieve the high yields that you can in the ground.

■ **HOW:** Source a large pot that's at least 16in x 20in (40cm x 50cm) deep with drainage holes and half fill with multipurpose compost. Space 1-2 chitted tubers on the surface and cover with 4in (10cm) of compost. Water and put in a sunny spot. Keep adding compost as the stems grow, until you almost get to the top of the pot. Keep well watered; give a liquid feed every 2 weeks.

February

THE EDIBLE GARDEN
- OTHER JOBS TO DO THIS MONTH

SOW

- Early broad beans such as 'Super Aquadulce' and early pea like 'Feltham First' outdoors. Also sow Brussels sprouts, kohl rabi and globe artichokes

PLANT OUT

- Onion and shallot sets outdoors for early crops. Spring garlic varieties if you have heavy wet winter soil

PRUNE

- Last chance to prune gooseberry and currant bushes while they are still dormant. Cut autumn raspberries back to the base

GENERAL TASKS

- **Hand-pollinate** peaches and apricots using a small paintbrush
- **Protect apricot** and peach blossom
- **Prune wall-trained figs** to encourage new fruit-bearing growth in spring
- **Order and plant out** bare-root bush tree and cane fruits, if you didn't last month

February project

Plant up an alpine container

ALPINES ARE fantastic plants, but they're often presumed to be too specialist for the average gardener. The truth is that many of these charming plants are easy to grow, as long as you give them sharp drainage and the right aspect.

Rockeries are the traditional way to display garden alpines, but not everybody has room for one. Every garden has space for an alpine container display, though, and by creating a 'miniature garden' in a trough or pot, you'll be able to appreciate the smallest, most intricate alpine varieties, up close.

TOP TIP
Place heavy stone troughs in their final position before planting up because they will be extremely heavy once planted

It's important to select compact plants that won't take over the container, and that all have similar growing requirements, be it full sun, dappled shade, or a cool spot.

Any wide, shallow container is fine as long as it has plenty of drainage holes in the bottom. Old stone sinks and hand-cast stone troughs are the traditional containers for alpines but these can be difficult to come across and costly. Garden centres usually stock a good range of imitation stone sinks or you could try making your own out of 'hypertufa' (a mix of coarse sand, Portland cement and peat or composted bark).

Step by step How to plant a trough

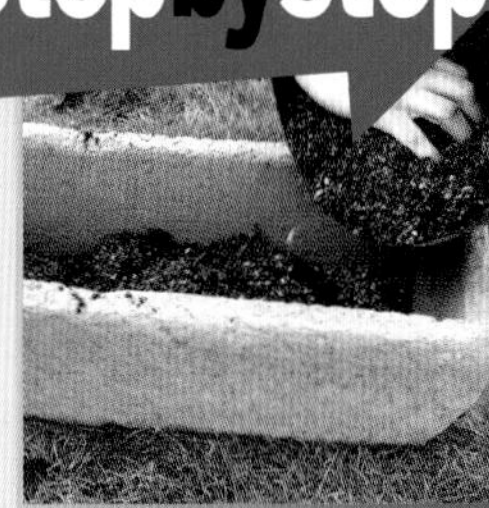

1 Put plenty of crocks at the base, covering drainage holes. Fill with 50:25:25 John Innes No1 potting compost, multipurpose compost and potting grit.

2 Stand your chosen alpines, still in their pots, on the surface and arrange them. Then tip them out and plant them so that they stand slightly proud of the compost.

3 Position chunks of rock or large stones, or set some pieces of slate on edge to mimic the natural rock strata normally found in mountainous regions.

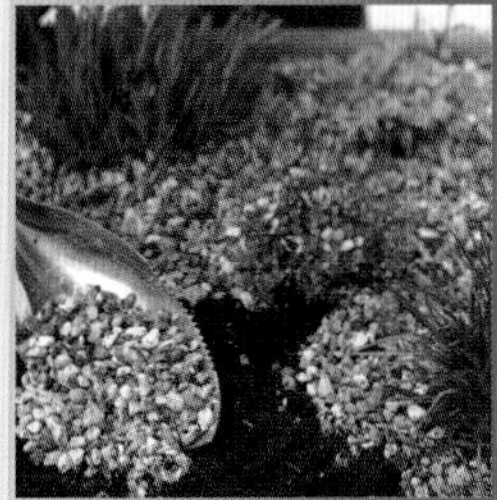

4 Cover the surface evenly with coarse or decorative gravel, to a depth of about half an inch. You could also use slate chips or coloured glass. Water in thoroughly.

WHAT TO PLANT

Choose plants that are evergreen and compact, so that your display will look good all year round. Contrast mound and rosette shapes with a few trailing kinds around the edges. The choice of alpines is vast; here are nine popular spring and summer varieties:

- **Gentiana verna** – striking sky-blue trumpet flowers in May/June (pic, above)
- **Narcissus minor** – charming dwarf daffodil with miniature yellow flowers
- **Sempervivum arachnoideum** – fleshy evergreen rosettes coated with white hairs; pink flowers in summer
- **Allium farreri** – umbels of starry plum-purple flowers in summer; 6in tall.
- **Picea glauca 'Alberta Globe'** – squat cone-shaped conifer
- **Saxifraga burseriana** – thick and spiny leaves, large white flowers on red stems Feb/March (pic, left)

- **Primula auricula 'Blairside yellow'** – yellow flowerheads, very small leaves
- **Saxifraga 'Knapton Pink'** – cushion-forming evergreen with small pink flowers on long stems in the spring
- **Delosperma 'Beaufort West'** – forms a dense mat, small star-shaped flowers

WINTER PROTECTION

- **Remove any leaves** that have fallen onto your alpines – they prevent light from reaching the plants and create damp conditions.

- **Even if you have used free-draining soil,** it still pays to protect your container over winter, as prolonged periods of rain could cause the plants to rot. An easy way to do this is to place two columns of bricks either side and lay a clear rigid plastic sheet over the top. Leave the sides uncovered to allow plenty of ventilation.

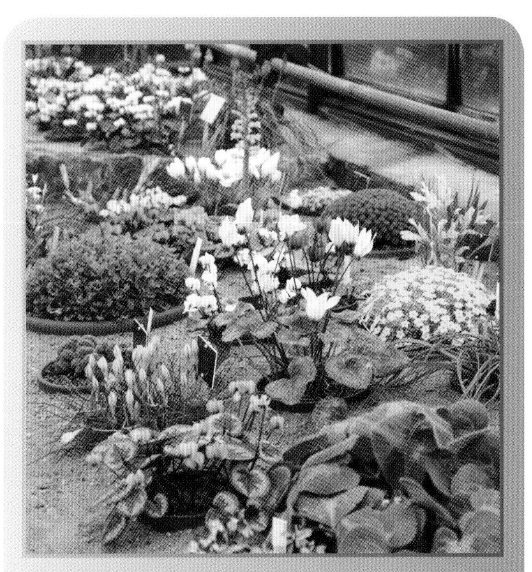

BECOME A COLLECTOR

Once you get into alpines, you'll be hooked! If you find yourself becoming an avid collector, consider turning your greenhouse into a dedicated 'Alpine House'. You'll be able to grow a more choice collection of alpines under the protection of glass. Ensure the greenhouse has ventilation and invest in special plunge trays filled with coarse sand to keep individual pots moist, humid and stable. There are lots of specialist books and societies, should you want to know more.

MARCH

Winter should be a dim and distant memory as spring officially gets underway, but it can often bite back, so continue to take special care of developing seedlings. You can add tomatoes, peppers and chillies to the sowing list, together with hardy annuals, while this is the month to plant summer-flowering bulbs such as gladiolus.

Pests are beginning to emerge, so decide whether you want to approach pest control organically or with chemical sprays, and be ready to take action.

Consider planting up a few patio pots with cheerful bedding plants for an extra boost of early spring colour.

MARCH PLANTS 5 OF THE BEST

1 PULMONARIA 'BLUE ENSIGN'

Excellent groundcover for a shady spot. Intense blue-violet flowers March-April. **H13in (35cm)**

2 VIBURNUM TINUS 'EVE PRICE'

Bright pink buds open to pinkish white flowerheads December to April. Glossy evergreen foliage adds structure to the garden. **H9½ft (3m)**

3

MAGNOLIA 'BLACK TULIP'

Striking magenta-pink cup-shaped flowers March to April. Underplant with spring bulbs for a stunning display. **H19ft (6m)**

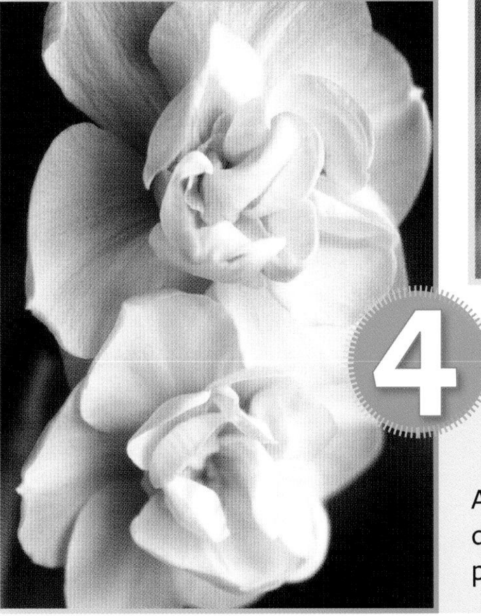

4

NARCISSUS 'CHEERFULNESS'

A superb March-flowering daffodil with creamy white double scented flowers; looks good mixed in with purple and yellow tulips. **H15in (37.5cm)**

5

CHAENOMELES SPECIOSA 'GEISHA GIRL'

Gorgeous pink-apricot flowers on bare branches brighten up the spring garden. An excellent shrub for sunny walls and hedging. **H8ft (2.5m)**

OTHERS TO TRY

- *Anemone blanda*
- *Bergenia* 'Eric Smith'
- *Camellia* 'Lemon Drop'
- *Clematis armandii*
- *Erysimum cheiri*
- *Magnolia stellata*
- *Muscari latifolium*
- *Narcissus* 'Jetfire'
- *Narcissus* 'Tête-à-tête'
- *Primula* 'Gold-laced Group'
- *Primula veris*
- *Tulipa fosteriana*

MARCH 2014

SATURDAY
1

SUNDAY
2

MONDAY
3

TUESDAY
4

WEDNESDAY
5

THURSDAY
6

FRIDAY
7

SATURDAY
8

AT A GLANCE
JOBS TO DO THIS MONTH

GENERAL TASKS

- ☐ Spruce up the garden – fork over borders, hoe weeds, cut back dead perennial stems left over the winter.
- ☐ Mulch the bare earth around plants with well-rotted manure if you haven't already done this in Jan/Feb.

LAWNS

- ☐ Begin regular mowing and edging the lawn, on dry days.
- ☐ Lay turf as the soil begins to warm, if you didn't in autumn.

TREES, SHRUBS AND CLIMBERS

- ☐ Last chance to get bare-root plants into the soil and to move deciduous trees and shrubs.
- ☐ Move evergreen shrubs.
- ☐ Plant new climbers.

FLOWERS

- ☐ Support herbaceous perennials.
- ☐ Sow hardy annuals.
- ☐ Divide overcrowded perennials.
- ☐ Divide/plant snowdrops in the green.
- ☐ Plant summer-flowering bulbs.

MARCH 2014

SUNDAY
9

MONDAY
10

TUESDAY
11

WEDNESDAY
12

THURSDAY
13

FRIDAY
14

SATURDAY
15

SUNDAY
16

Plant gladioli corms now

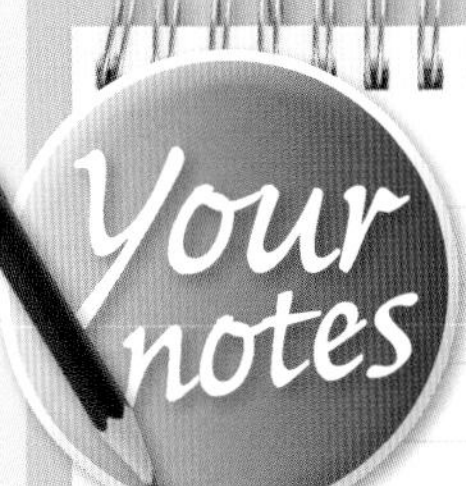

WEATHER:

PLANTS IN BLOOM:

TO DO:

MARCH 2014

MONDAY
17

TUESDAY
18

WEDNESDAY
19

THURSDAY
20

FRIDAY
21

SATURDAY
22

SUNDAY
23

MONDAY
24

AT A GLANCE
JOBS TO DO THIS MONTH

IN THE GREENHOUSE

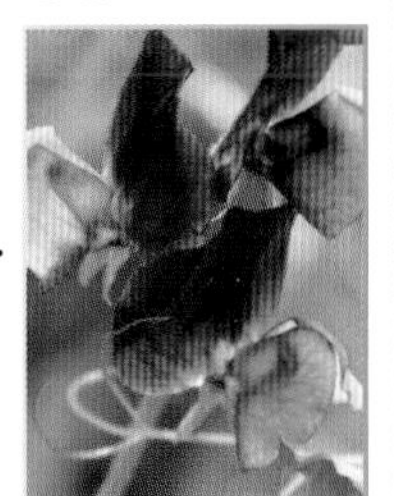

- ☐ Sow sweet peas if you didn't get around to it in January or February.
- ☐ Pot up plug plants and young plants after delivery or purchase.
- ☐ Repot cacti and succulents. Start off dahlias if you didn't last month; take cuttings from sprouting tubers. On cold nights cover vulnerable plants with newspaper or fleece.

CONTAINERS AND PATIOS

- ☐ Plant/freshen up seasonal containers with spring bedding, small evergreens and compact perennials; use John Innes No3 compost in long-term containers, multipurpose in short-term ones.
- ☐ Spruce up the the patio by giving it a good scrub and removing moss and weeds.

WHAT TO PRUNE

- **Coppice recently planted eucalyptus to encourage it to grow into a shrub**
- **Prune bush and shrub roses**
- **Cut back coloured stems of dogwood and salix hard**
- **Renovate climbers by cutting them back hard**

MARCH 2014

TUESDAY
25

WEDNESDAY
26

THURSDAY
27

FRIDAY
28

SATURDAY
29

SUNDAY
30

MONDAY
31

Divide snowdrop clumps in the green

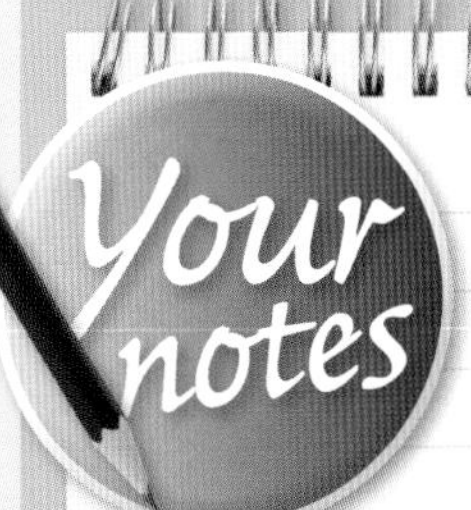

WEATHER:

PLANTS IN BLOOM:

TO DO:

Focus on evergreens

March and April are key months for moving and planting evergreen shrubs. If evergreens are moved in the depth of winter, it's unlikely they'll be able to replace the water lost from their leaves through wind and frost, and plants don't generally take up water when the soil is cold.

Similarly, it's best to plant out pot-grown evergreens in spring when the temperature is on the increase and plants are starting to put on growth. Don't leave it until summer: evergreen shrubs are woody and need lots of watering to get established. If you do miss the spring window, wait until autumn – which is the other ideal time to plant and move evergreens.

TOP TIP
Hard frost and winds can lift newly planted shrubs – simply heel them back in again if this happens

Evergreens have so many uses in the garden. At the formal end of the spectrum, they make excellent hedging, defining boundaries, providing privacy and creating shelter. In the borders, several evergreen shrubs dotted through softer perennials and annuals add in a 'backbone'. At the smaller end of the scale dwarf conifer and pine varieties sit well in containers, and topiary in pots is an attractive way to frame a doorway. In winter, when most other plants have died down, evergreens give the garden structure.

Stepbystep Planting evergreens

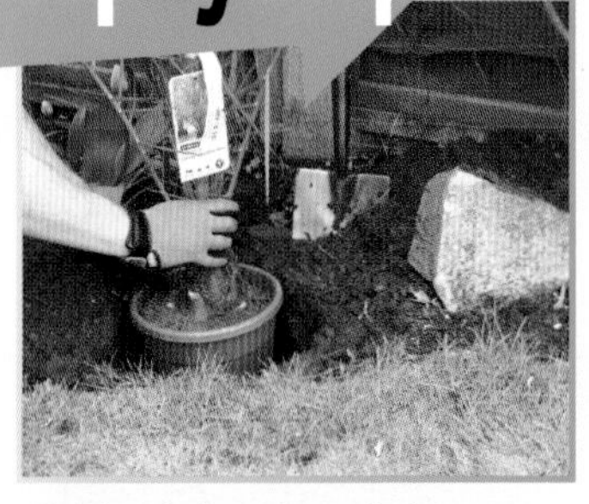

1 Dig a hole not much deeper than the plant's pot, but twice as wide. Test the depth by placing the pot in the hole, digging out more or replacing the soil to suit.

2 Remove the plant from its pot and tease some of the dense roots away from the rootball. This will speed up establishment and help roots to anchor into the soil.

3 Backfill and firm in the rootball making sure the top of it is level with the soil surface. Water thoroughly. Mulch around the base to preserve moisture.

FEEDING

You only need to feed newly planted evergreens for the first couple of years after planting; established evergreens don't need regular feeding.

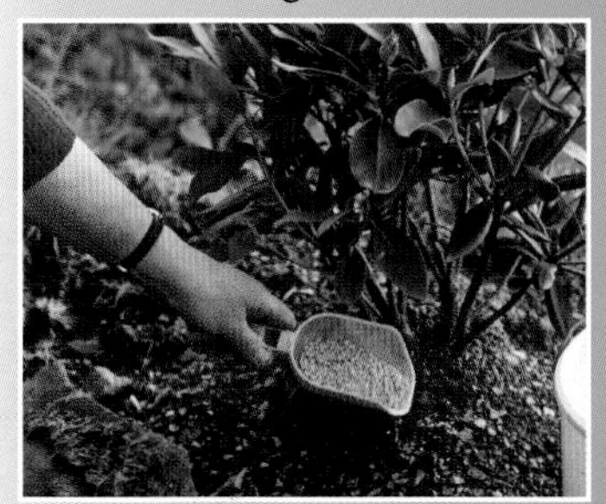

Scatter organic fertiliser like blood, fish and bone around the base of plants in February, or a synthetic (faster acting) feed in April.

PRUNING

Once established, evergreen plants need little or no regular pruning – but do keep an eye out for dead, diseased or damaged branches.

If pruning is required, spring is the time to do it, but prune flowering hedges immediately after flowering.

Evergreen hedges need regular pruning throughout the growing season to keep them dense and compact. Pruning times vary depending on the type of evergreen hedge – but most require two or three trims from April to September.

MOVING

Now is the ideal time to lift established plants and replant them elsewhere in the garden. Here's how to do it:

- Dig a trench around the plant to be moved, a few inches out from the canopy edge, a spade's spit wide and around 12in (30cm) deep.

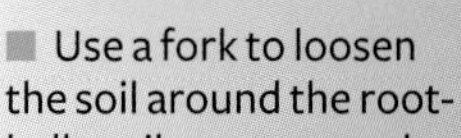

- Use a fork to loosen the soil around the rootball until you expose the edge of the roots, aiming to cause as little damage as possible.

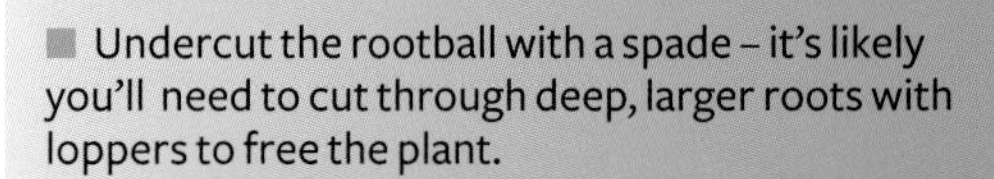

- Undercut the rootball with a spade – it's likely you'll need to cut through deep, larger roots with loppers to free the plant.

- Lift the rootball on to polythene sheeting, damp hessian or old towels. Wrap the root ball and lift to the new planting site.

FIVE TOP EVERGREENS

1 Hebe 'Heartbreaker'

Mounds of slender cream-edged leaves that take on a pink tint when the temperature drops. Mauve-coloured summer flowers. Great for a small garden or pot. **H2ft (60cm)**

2 Viburnum davidii

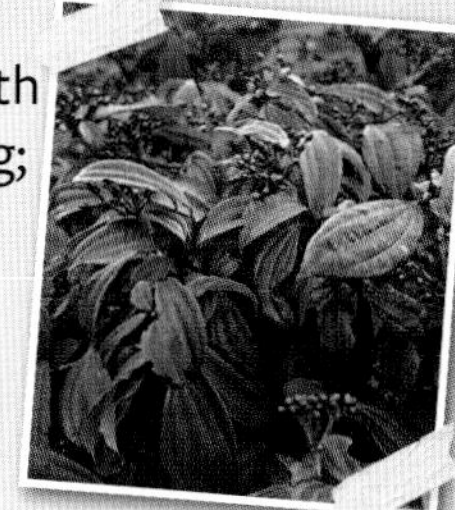

Attractive compact groundcover plant for front of border. Leaves with prominent veining; white flowers in May followed by purple berries. **H4½ft (1.5m)**

3 Prunus laurocerasus 'Rotundifolia'

Ideal hedging plant. Bushy, fast-growing. Will cope with deep shade as well as full sun. Can be clipped as a specimen shrub, too. **H16ft (5m)**

4 Buxus sempervirens

Slow-growing box, excellent for hedging and topiary. Best in partial shade and compost must never dry out. **H9ft (3m)**

5 Choisya x dewitteana 'Aztec Pearl'

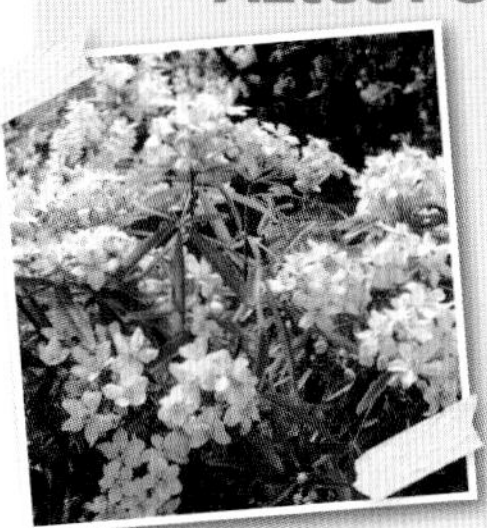

More compact than C. *ternata*. An elegant shrub with narrow dark-green foliage and fragrant white flowers in May. **H8ft (2.5m)**

Prune bush & shrub roses

The best time to prune roses is late winter/early spring just as they're starting into growth. Depending on where you are in the country and weather conditions, this could be any time between February and April. We're talking about shrub and bush roses here – ramblers and climbers are best pruned in autumn (see pp158-159).

Bush roses are either floribunda or hybrid teas – the latter have long stems and cone-shaped flowers, while in contrast, the floribundas bear their flowers in clusters. Both are pruned quite harshly.

Shrub roses produce many stems and have a more informal, shrub-like habit, and are only lightly pruned. They tend to be appreciated for the overall look they give rather than their individual blooms, which can be single, semi-double, or double.
The main reason to prune roses is to keep them healthy and flowering well.

It's another of those gardening tasks that many feel daunted by, but it really is a lot more straightforward than you think.

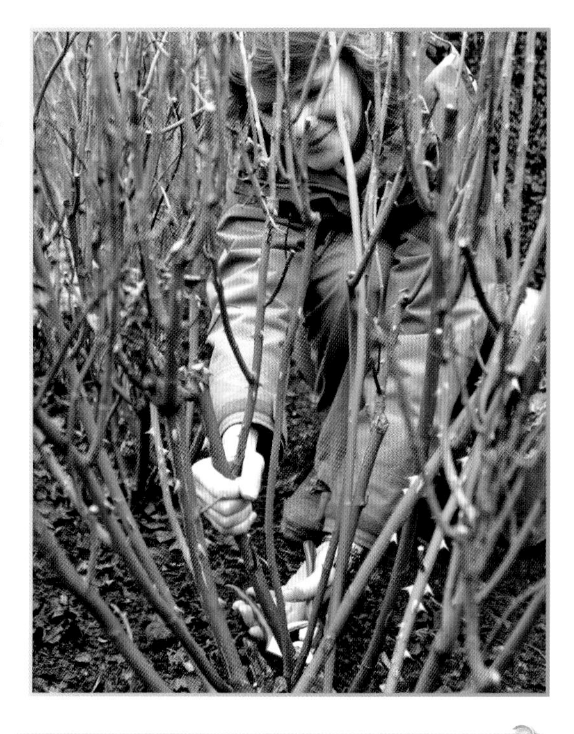

QUICK GUIDE ROSES TO PRUNE NOW

Always aim to create an open structure to reduce the chance of rose fungal diseases. Remove the three Ds – dead, diseased and dying

- **Bush roses (Hybrid tea, floribunda and patio roses)** – cut stems back to about half, leave them slightly longer for floribundas.
- **Shrub roses** – reduce healthy main stems by about a quarter. Thin out.
- **Groundcover** – reduce congestion by removing some of the thicker branches.
- **Miniatures** – shorten any weak growth.

BASIC ANNUAL CARE

Roses are hungry plants and will benefit from a fertiliser boost every spring

Feed

Sprinkle a general rose fertiliser around the base of plants in spring. Repeat in summer if growth is slow.

Mulch

Follow feeding immediately with a mulch of well-rotted manure, if possible.

Water

Water plants during dry spells, especially new plants; dry soil around the roots encourages powdery mildew.

Step by step How to prune roses

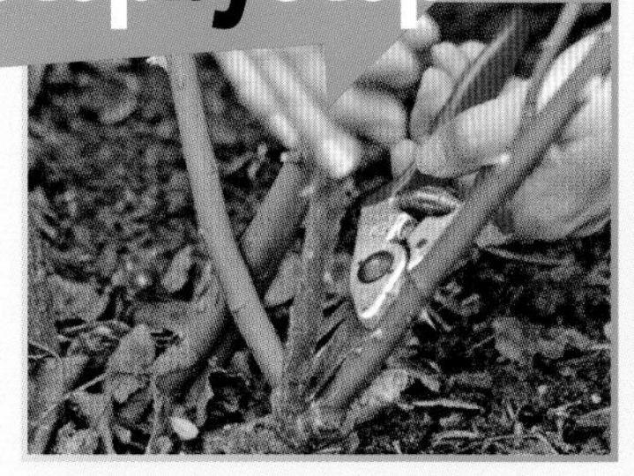

1 Stand back from your rose to assess its shape and what needs pruning. Remove dead, diseased and dying stems.

2 Cut just above an outward-facing bud, so that new growth develops outwards. Slant cuts downwards away from buds.

3 Bush roses are pruned quite harshly: aim to reduce them by about half. Reduce shrub roses by about a quarter.

Last chance

This month is your last chance to plant out bare-root roses. If you've missed the spring window, bare-roots will become available again in autumn. Pot-grown roses are available all year round, however they do need lots of water after planting. When purchasing, consider whether you want a repeat-flowerer (generally these flower on and off until September) or a once-and-only rose that will give a 3-week profuse display in June.

PEST & DISEASE WATCH

When pruning your roses watch out for the following pests and diseases

Aphids – squash between finger and thumb

Rose sawfly – where infestations are light, pick off affected foliage

Black spot – destroy and burn affected foliage

Rose rust – destroy and burn affected foliage

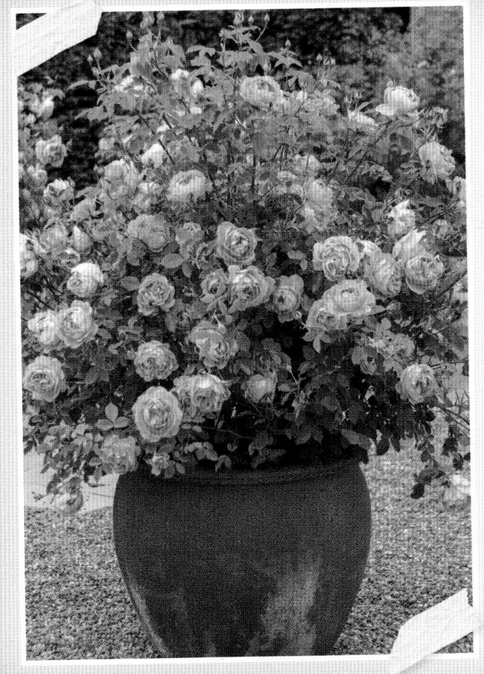

PLANTING IN CONTAINERS

Variety selection is important when it comes to choosing a rose for container planting, as some will not perform well in the confines of a pot. Ask garden centre staff for advice but as a general rule, choose a patio or miniature variety. Some shrub roses like David Austin's 'Lady of Shalott' (pictured) are suitable for large pots.

Use the biggest container you can find (minimum depth 12in/30cm) and fill with a loam-based John Innes No3 compost.

Every spring, remove the top few inches of compost and replace with fresh. Apply a top dressing of granular fertiliser.

Sow hardy annuals

Hardy annuals are an easy way to fill the borders with colour. There's no messing about with pricking out, potting on and hardening off – you simply sow them direct into the soil.

When you choose to do this is a matter of choice. Some gardeners swear by autumn-sowing so that plants will form healthy rootballs over the winter months and then romp away quickly in spring when the hours of daylight and temperatures increase. Others, particularly those in cold, wet parts of the country, prefer to wait until spring, when the soil is warming up for the season ahead.

There's a huge range of hardy annuals to choose from, something to suit all tastes and styles, so you can easily put on a really good display of colour this summer for little money. Use them to fill gaps in the borders between permanent perennial and shrub plantings, or devote an area especially to them.

PREPARE THE SOIL WELL

On a dry day, two or three weeks before you plan to sow your hardy annuals, dig the soil over adding in plenty of organic matter such as well-rotted manure. Sprinkle over handfuls of general-purpose fertiliser at the manufacturer's recommended rate. Then rake the soil to a fine tilth, to create a texture that resembles cake crumbs. Hardy annual seed is often small and fine, and seedlings will struggle to push their way through large lumps of soil.

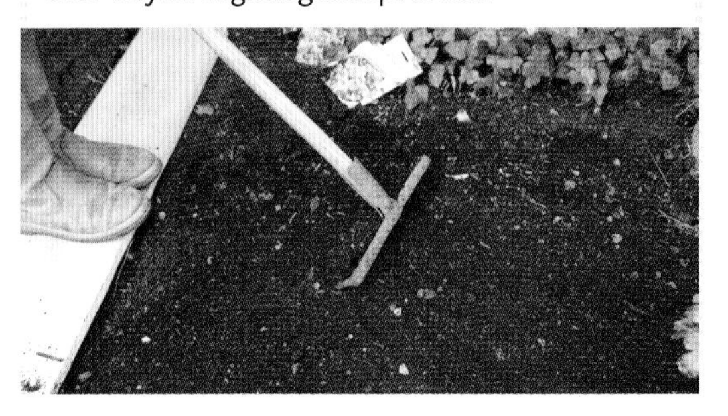

BROADCAST VS DRILL SOWING

Broadcast sowing brings the most natural look to annual flower displays. This means scattering your chosen seeds over the surface. Start at the back of the area to be sown and work to the front. A disadvantage of this type of sowing is that it is difficult to spot emerging weeds among the seedlings. A good compromise is to mark out sweeping drifts to give the impression of natural look, then drill sow within each drift.

Step by step How to sow

1 In prepared soil, use sand to mark out drifts. Check the height and spread of the plants, sowing taller varieties at the back.

2 Mark out shallow drills using a cane. Set drills in different directions for each area, then sow seed thinly along each drill.

3 Gently rake soil over the seeds. Label drifts and water in the area. Cover with fleece to prevent disturbance if cats are a problem.

TOP 7 HARDY ANNUALS

1 ***Eschscholzia californica*** – Californian Poppies look great in coastal or dry themed borders

2 ***Nigella damascena* 'Moody Blues'** – grow love-in the-mist in big clumps for dramatic effect

3 ***Limnanthes douglasii*** – the poached egg plant is loved by pollinators

4 ***Orlaya grandiflora*** – summer-flowering beauty with fern-like foliage

5 ***Echium vulgare* 'Blue Bedder'** – viper's bugloss is a magnet to bees and other beneficial insects

6 ***Papaver somniferum*** – the opium poppy is grown for its striking seed heads as much as the crimson flowers

7 ***Nasturtium* 'Troika'** – looks great in hanging baskets

Grow your own tomatoes

Homegrown tomatoes are one of the delights of the summer veg garden: when picked perfectly ripe, they beat shop-bought ones hands down.

The seeds can be sown anytime from mid-January to early April, and they normally take 6-8 weeks after germination to form plants that are big enough to plant into their final positions.

Coming from warm-climate countries, tomatoes must be kept frost-free at all times, so only sow early in the year if you have the facilities to keep plants undercover in light, frost-free conditions, and only plant out when all threat of frost has passed.

The job of getting tomatoes to ripen successfully outdoors in the UK climate is a bit hit and miss, and results are normally much better when they're grown under glass. That said, if you get lucky with the weather, tomatoes ripened by direct sun have a wonderful rich flavour.

There's a wide range of varieties available – from tried and trusted old favourites through to more unusual, exotic and rare types.

Generally, tomatoes split into two distinct groups: vine (indeterminate) and bush (determinate). As the name suggests, bush types are compact plants, perfect for patio pots and smaller gardens; they tend to crop early, with fruits ripening all at the same time. There's a wider choice with vine tomatoes, but they will need staking, tying in, and pinching out.

Whether you choose bush or vine varieties, the method for sowing the seeds is the same.

TOP TIP
If you've missed the spring sowing window or prefer not to grow from seed, plenty of garden centres sell young tomato plants

Step by step: How to sow tomato seed

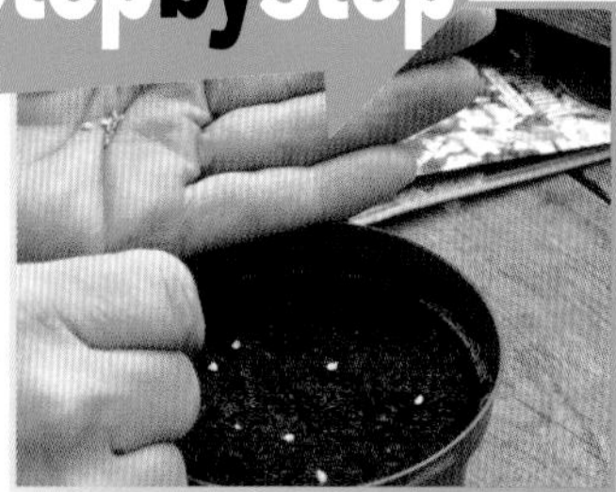

1 Sow seeds in pots or tray on the surface of damp seed compost, spaced about a finger-width apart. Cover with a thin layer of vermiculite.

2 Ideally place the pots or trays into a heated propagator; if this is not possible place them in clear plastic bags on a sunny indoor windowsill.

3 Seedlings should emerge within two weeks, and after another two weeks they should be large enough to prick out and pot up in individual pots.

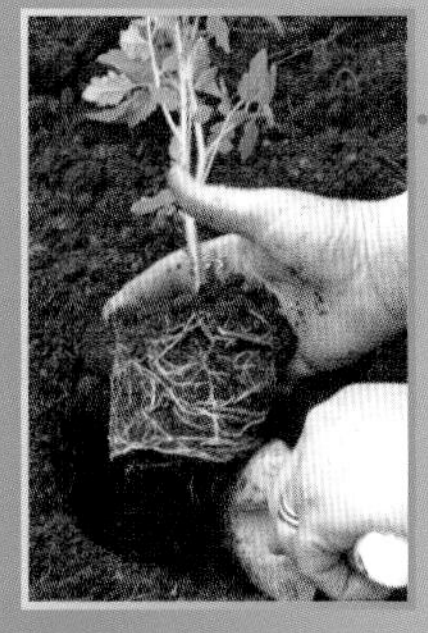

PLANT OUT

Plant outdoors in early summer in a sunny, sheltered spot, into soil that's been enriched with plenty of compost or well-rotted manure. If growing under glass, plant mid-spring. Set plants 16in (40cm) apart.

TIE IN, PINCH OUT

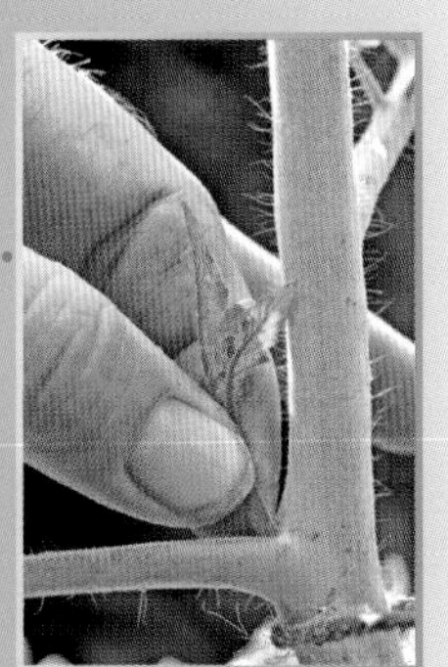

Support plants by tying stems to a cane. When vine tomatoes have six sets of trusses (the flowering branches) – four for outdoor types – cut off the top of plants. Pinch out any shoots that develop between stem and main branches.

ROUTINE CARE

Feeding isn't essential for soil-grown plants but those in pots and growing bags will need a regular feed, every two weeks or so. Water the soil not the plant – tomatoes don't like their foliage getting wet.

HARVEST

If any fruits are shy to ripen, pick and place them next to a banana – the ethylene from the banana helps them to ripen.

March

THE EDIBLE GARDEN
- OTHER JOBS TO DO THIS MONTH

SOW

- Start regular sowings of herbs, lettuce, cauliflower, beetroot, early carrots, calabrese, broad beans, peppers and chillies

PLANT

- Early potatoes in the ground or in bags, onions, shallots, young peas, rhubarb, pot-grown fruit, strawberry plants

GENERAL TASKS

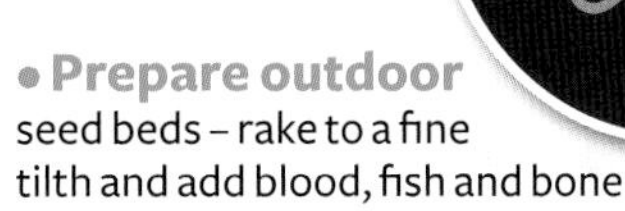

- **Prepare outdoor** seed beds – rake to a fine tilth and add blood, fish and bone
- **Divide chives** and other overcrowded perennial herbs
- **Weed the veg patch** – hoe off annual weeds and rigorously dig out perennials

VARIETIES TO TRY

- 'Sungold' – exceptionally sweet, orange-red fruits
- 'Costoluto Fiorentino' – juicy Italian vine variety
- 'Gardener's Delight' – an old favourite. Cherry bite-sized tangy tomatoes

March project

Grow salad all year round

IT'S POSSIBLE to grow and eat mouthwatering salad from January to December. Our year planner details top varieties to grow each season, as well as basic cultivation details.

The secret to growing great tasting salad is to add lots of enriching organic matter like well-rotted manure and garden compost to the soil bed before planting out and to keep on top of weeds and slugs.

Raise seedlings indoors in trays and modules to avoid slugs eating them, then plant at about four weeks old to ensure a good root system. Avoid overwatering, especially in cloudy and cool weather, as a dry surface reduces slug and downy mildew damage.

You don't need to harvest entire lettuce plants: plant them 10in (25cm) apart and allow to grow until the leaves almost touch, then twist off outer and larger leaves weekly, keeping plants in a state of adolescence for up to three months.

YEAR PLANNER

Winter

LAMB'S LETTUCE 'Pulsar' and 'D'Orlanda' resist all frost

LAND CRESS So hardy and full of flavour (pictured, right)

WINTER PURSLANE Tender leaves are frost hardy but will discolour in deep cold

KALE 'Red Russian' for a few tender new leaves

ENDIVE 'Bubikopf', along with Spinach 'Medania' and Chard 'Five Colour', are best cloched

MUSTARD 'Green in the Snow' is pungent and hardy

SALAD ROCKET Keeps going in mild winters

MIZUNA Ideally protect with horticultural fleece

PARSLEY Will endure winter well – especially curled varieties – and give small new leaves

KEEP LEAVES COMING

Sow parsley and kale in July, land cress, spinach, endive in August, then lamb's lettuce, winter purslane, rocket, mustard, mizuna in late August. There will be some pickings from October until December when plants go semi-dormant. Any cover will help them grow.

Spring

LETTUCE 'Freckles', 'Bijou', 'Lettony', 'Maravilla de Verono Canasta' and 'Lollo Rossa' are all good for regular picking of outer leaves (right)

PEA SHOOTS Sow thickly in rows or in pots; keep picking the new shoots for 6-8 weeks

SPINACH Pick the dark green leaves of 'Toscane F1' for 6-8 weeks before flowering

SORREL (Large-leaved) Pick the young leaves of this perennial for a taste of lemon

WILD ROCKET Harvest leaves from April, from overwintered plants sown the previous autumn

KALE The young shoots and new leaves are tender and sweet until final flowering in May; sow in summer

GETTING STARTED

The majority of spring seeds should be sown indoors in February, for planting out in March and April, or first outdoor sowings late March. Use fleece covers to help early growth. Sorrel and overwintered salads start cropping early, while first harvests from seed-sown plants begin in late April.

Summer

LETTUCE Varieties as spring; sow early June for picking from mid July through to autumn

TREE SPINACH Only one plant needed for a succession of pretty magenta shoots until September

BUCKLER LEAF SORREL Perennial that will provide a steady growth of leaves with lemony taste

WILD ROCKET From autumn sowings the previous year, continues growing but becomes thinner leaved

BASIL Select sweet, lemon and cinnamon varieties for deep flavours; best grown under cover

PETALS Marigold 'Golden Gem', *Calendula officinalis* and nasturtium are easy to grow and give welcome colour (eat petals only)

CARROT LEAF 'AMSTERDAM' fine-leaved variety of carrot; only pick leaves when young

WATERCRESS 'AQUA' Watercress you can grow without running water. Sow from mid-May. Keep compost moist and plants shaded

TOP TIPS

Sow lettuce late May to early June so it starts to give leaves in July when the spring lettuce is rising to flower. Sow tree spinach in March under cover or April outside; sow annual flowers in April and May. Sow basil undercover in April and grow in the warmest, most sheltered spot you have. Wild rocket and sorrel need frequent picking to reduce flowering.

Autumn

LETTUCE 'Maravilla de Verano Canasta' and 'Grenoble Red' are two varieties that resist mildew; sow mid July

ENDIVE Choose 'Frenzy' and 'Bianca Riccia da Taglio' for green and yellow respectively. 'Bubikopf' grows well in the cold: sow August and pick as you would leaf lettuce

SALAD ROCKET Grows superbly all autumn, from sowings in early August. It has larger, juicier, faster-growing leaves than wild rocket

MUSTARDS 'Red Frills', 'Red Dragon' and 'Pizzo' add fire and colour; they're also fast to grow and abundant

MIZUNA A mild-flavoured leaf offering a cool balance to the mustards. Extremely fast-growing, sow as late as early September

LAND CRESS Tolerates all weathers; grow for a tasty, hot, watercress-like flavour

CHERVIL & CORIANDER These herbs grow abundantly in autumn and give wonderful flavour to salads

WHEN TO SOW

For less mildew problems and more leaves in colder weather, grow endive more than lettuce. Sow it in July's second half along with land cress, chervil and coriander to provide leaves through autumn. The other salads are fast growers. Best sown in August, plants will be healthy and vigorous until the first hard frost, with regular pickings all through autumn.

APRIL

Lighter evenings and milder days mean there are more opportunities to get out into the garden. Don't be lulled into a false sense of security, though, as frosts are still common in April.

The mower blades can be lowered and lawn sand applied if moss is a problem. Outdoor tomatoes, cucumbers and courgettes should be sown now, together with successional sowings of lettuce, beans and peas. You can also sow onions, winter cabbage and carrots.

Prick out indoor-sown seedlings as soon as they are big enough to handle – but keep them out of direct sunlight. Second early and maincrop potatoes should also be planted in April.

APRIL PLANTS
5 OF THE BEST

1 AMELANCHIER LAMARCKII

These small trees offer two seasons of interest – white star blossom and bronze-tinted foliage in spring, and green summer leaves that turn coppery red in autumn. **H16ft (5m)**

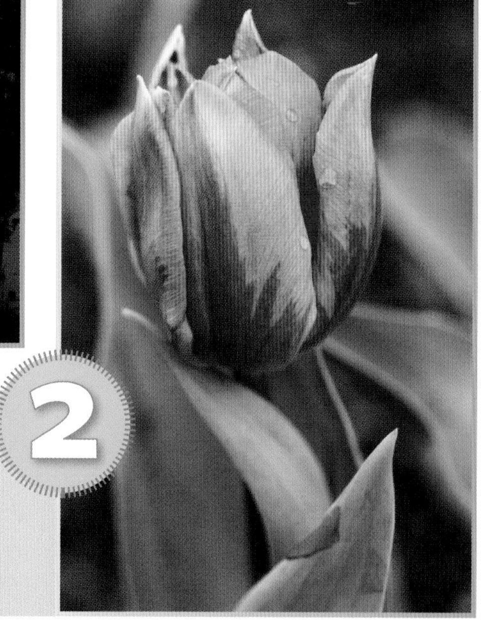

2 TULIPA 'PRINSES IRENE'

Soft-orange blooms, flushed purple are sweetly scented. Looks lovely in a terracotta pot with *Narcissus* 'Minnow'. **H1ft (30cm)**

3 VINCA MAJOR 'VARIEGATA'

A useful bright, variegated groundcover that lifts any shady spot out of the gloom. Purple flowers appear in spring and last until September. **H18in (45cm)**

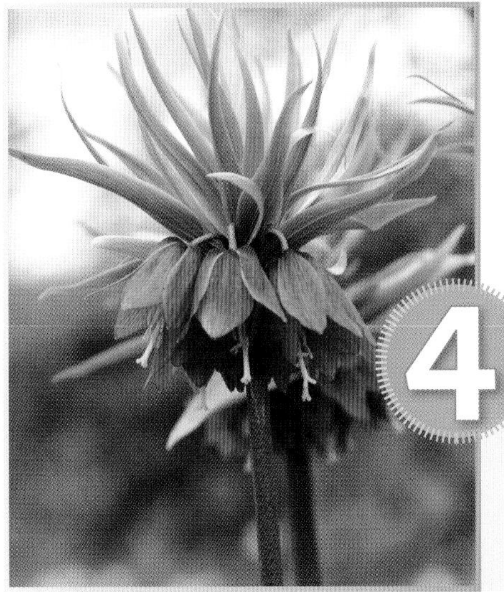

4 FRITILLARIA IMPERIALIS

Crown fritillaries are one of the joys of spring – unmissable in the borders. The secret to growing them successfully is to plant them on their sides. **H3ft (1m)**

5 LAMPROCAPNOS SPECTABILIS

Magnificent arching stems dripping with heart-shaped blooms from April to June. A must-have spring perennial for shade or sun. **H47in (1.2m)**

OTHERS TO TRY

- *Acer* 'Emerald Lace'
- *Akebia quinata*
- *Berberis darwinii*
- *Clematis* 'Lemon Dream'
- *Dicentra* 'Bacchanal'
- *Epimedium x warleyense*
- *Euphorbia x martinii*
- *Photinia x fraseri* 'Red Robin'
- *Pieris* 'Forest Flame'
- *Prunus* 'Kiku-shidare-zakura'
- *Pulsatilla vulgaris*
- *Rhododendron* 'Azuma-kagami'

APRIL 2014

TUESDAY
1

WEDNESDAY
2

THURSDAY
3

FRIDAY
4

SATURDAY
5

SUNDAY
6

MONDAY
7

TUESDAY
8

AT A GLANCE
JOBS TO DO THIS MONTH

GENERAL TASKS

- ☐ Slugs and other pests will start to come in force this month – keep on top of them.
- ☐ Apply a light dressing of fertiliser such as blood, fish and bone around the borders.
- ☐ Keep borders ticking over – fork over, weed and hoe.

LAWNS

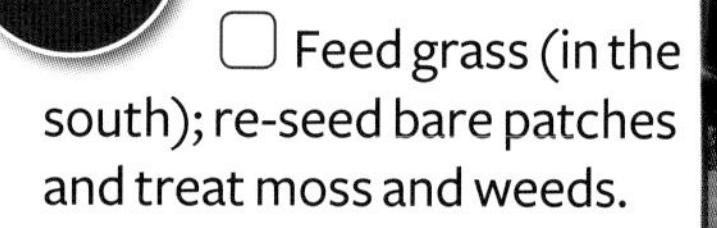

- ☐ Feed grass (in the south); re-seed bare patches and treat moss and weeds.
- ☐ Mow lawns at least once a fortnight; keep up with edging.
- ☐ Sow grass seed for a new lawn if you can't wait until autumn.

TREES, SHRUBS AND CLIMBERS

- ☐ Continue to plant or move evergreens.
- ☐ Continue to plant container-grown woody plants.
- ☐ Tie-in climbing roses, wall-trained shrubs and newly planted climbers.

APRIL 2014

WEDNESDAY

9

THURSDAY

10

FRIDAY

11

SATURDAY

12

SUNDAY

13

MONDAY

14

TUESDAY

15

WEDNESDAY

16

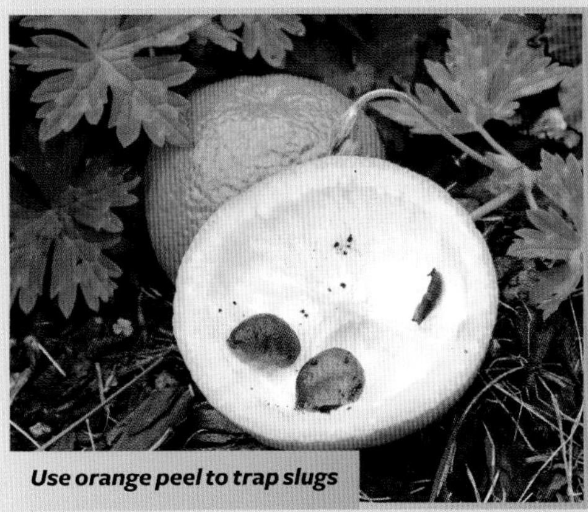

Use orange peel to trap slugs

WEATHER:

PLANTS IN BLOOM:

TO DO:

APRIL 2014

THURSDAY
17

FRIDAY
18

SATURDAY
19

SUNDAY
20

MONDAY
21

TUESDAY
22

WEDNESDAY
23

THURSDAY
24

AT A GLANCE
JOBS TO DO THIS MONTH

FLOWERS

- ☐ Keep planting and dividing perennials.
- ☐ Deadhead daffodil flowers.
- ☐ Plant summer bulbs and *Anemone* de Caen in borders or containers.
- ☐ Sow hardy annuals direct (in the north).
- ☐ Sow sweet peas direct (in the south).

IN THE GREENHOUSE

- ☐ Start hardening off summer bedding during the day.
- ☐ Pot up rooted cuttings from last year.
- ☐ Pot on begonias.
- ☐ Buy and pot up plug plants.
- ☐ Plant up a hanging basket and keep it under protection.

CONTAINERS & PATIOS

- ☐ Remove winter protection from pots.
- ☐ Plant spring bedding in containers.

- **Forsythia**
- **Chaenomeles**
- **Lavender (pictured)**
- **Sambucus and cotinus (for foliage)**
- **Hydrangea**
- **Winter jasmine**

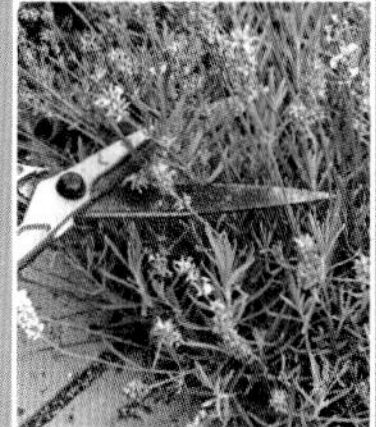

APRIL 2014

FRIDAY
25

SATURDAY
26

SUNDAY
27

MONDAY
28

TUESDAY
29

WEDNESDAY
30

Plant Anemone de caen corms

WEATHER:

PLANTS IN BLOOM:

TO DO:

10-step lawn plan

As we move into spring it's time to start thinking about our lawn care regime for the season.

Late February to early May is a key time for carrying out lawn maintenance, before the grass (and weeds) start to romp away. With a good-looking lawn the garden can look presentable, even if the beds and borders don't stand up to scrutiny!

Over the past few weeks you may have noticed worm casts appearing across the lawn. This is more often than not a problem on cold, shady plots and is the first sign that some attention needs to be given to the lawn in order to get it in shape for this coming year.

Follow this 10-step plan and get your lawn looking smart for the season ahead.

1 WORM CASTS

To avoid smearing the casts into the lawn, wait for them to dry out before sweeping them in with a stiff brush; they are nutrient-rich and provide good compost for the lawn. However, wormcasts can be a sign that the lawn is waterlogged.

2 AERATION

If waterlogging has been a problem over winter, deep aeration (below 3in/7.5cm) using a fork or motorised spiker is the solution. This is worth doing on all lawns. Follow spiking by top-dressing with John Innes No3 compost. Sweep it into the spike holes.

3 FIRST CUT

Mild weather can cause grass to put on growth, so keep the lawnmower maintained in readiness. In a mild winter this may mean cutting even in December or January. The season's first cut should consist of a light trim, so set the mower blades high. Don't cut the lawn when it's wet, to avoid compaction.

4 NEW LAWNS

Autumn is the ideal time to lay new turf, but if you're unable to lay one until spring, it should be done by early April. Unlike autumn laying, a new spring lawn will have to be backed up with heavy watering to ensure it survives through its first summer. Similarly, sowing a new lawn from seed will need a little more attention at this time of year and will take up to two weeks longer before shoots start to appear.

5 RAKING

A spring-tine rake is an essential tool if you want a good-looking lawn. In autumn the rake is used forcefully to remove thatch (dead grass) from the lawn, but a lighter approach is needed in spring to remove any thatch and debris missed in autumn.

6 MOSS CONTROL

Traditionally, a topdressing of lawn sand is used to control moss in lawns: the added sulphate of iron in the sand causes the moss to burn off. Sprinkle handfuls of the sand evenly over the affected area, following the manufacturer's application rate, then water into the lawn or wait for rain to do the job for you. The dead moss then needs to be raked off the lawn. These are autumn jobs but if moss is a problem do not wait to tackle it.

7 EDGING

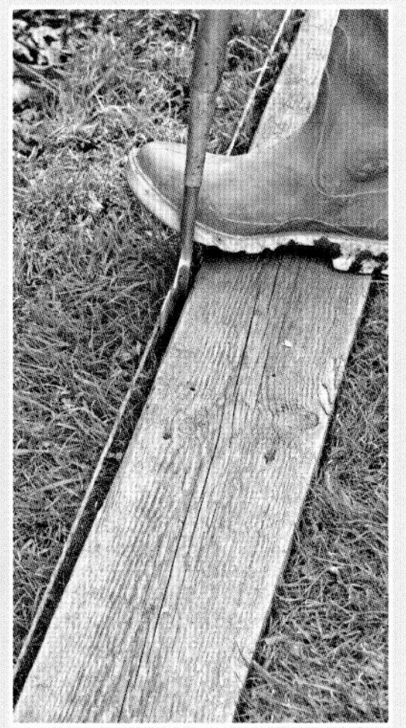

A lawn with overgrown edges is a real eyesore. If the standard of the current edges is sound, with good vertical sides, then all you will need to do is to give the edges a trim with a pair of sharp edging shears. However, if the edges have collapsed or been worn down in places, then you need to use a half-moon edging iron to cut and create new vertical sides. A plank of wood is useful as a guide and is handy to stand on if the soil is damp.

8 PATCHES

Fill in patchy areas by raking out any dead growth and titivating the uncovered soil. New seed can then by sown across the space. Getting perfect results can be a challenge, particularly in shady or sunny spots.

9 WEEDS

Broadleaf weeds such as dandelions and daisies can quickly be brought under control with a selective lawn weedkiller. Make sure the product you buy is designed for specific use with lawns, otherwise big problems could occur. If you're organic, regularly removed perennial weeds with a narrow trowel; encourage clover as its nitrogen-fixing roots act to feed the soil.

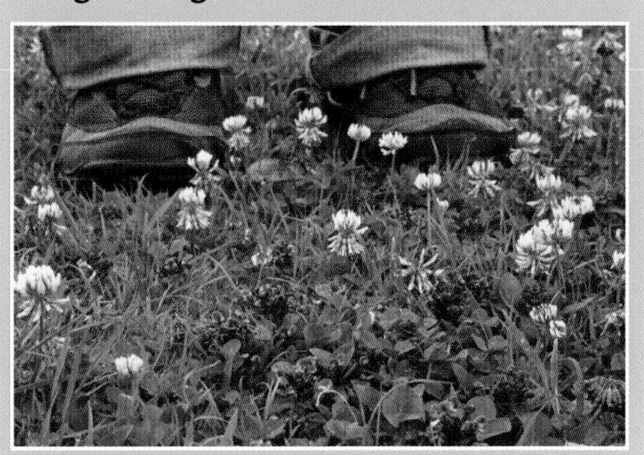

10 FEEDING

Feeding your lawn will help the grass to stay healthy, lush and green throughout the year, but the right lawn feed is crucial for good results. Look for spring feeds with a high concentration of nitrogen to encourage vigorous leaf growth and good colour. A slow release granular feed is better than liquid and water-soluble feeds, as the rain can easily wash these away.

Grow annual climbers

Much like hardy annuals, annual climbers are another quick and easy way to fill the garden with a riot of colour – only this time, vertically.

They're great for covering bare fences and softening walls, and are easy to grow up obelisks and wigwams to provide vertical interest in the borders. You can even use them to scramble through spring-flowering shrubs that end up looking a bit dull in the summer, such as forsythia. And if you grow them up supports in large containers they can brighten up patio and conservatories.

The majority of annual climbers are perennial plants in their warm native countries – we treat them as half-hardy annuals as they won't survive a UK winter outdoors.

They need a long growing season to produce flowers just when we want them, in high summer, so ideally, start them off in February. If you don't want to sow seeds as early as February, you could wait until the weather warms up in April and sow for slightly later flowering plants.

TOP TIP
If growing in a container, move into a frost-free greenhouse or conservatory at the end of summer to enjoy the blooms well into autumn

Another way to grow annual climbers is with climbing vegetables – this is really great way to make the veg plot look pretty: try training baby squash and pumpkins with flowering climbers up a sturdy frame, for instance.

Stepbystep How to sow

1 Sow seeds on the surface of damp compost and cover with a thin layer of compost. Ideally place in a heated propagator; but you can cover with a clear plastic bag and keep on a warm windowsill.

2 After germination, remove covers. When seedlings are large enough to handle, fill small pots with multipurpose compost, dib planting holes and set single plants or trios in place.

3 To keep plants tidy and catch the first 'clinging' growth, set a few skewers or pea sticks in the compost close to the seedlings. Water in and keep on a bright windowsill or in a greenhouse.

VARIETIES TO TRY

1 ***Cobaea scandens*** **(cup and saucer plant)** – the pale green scented bell-shaped flowers turn to purple as they age.

2 ***Ipomoea lobata*** **(Spanish flag)** – racemes of red flowers, turning to orange, yellow and white.

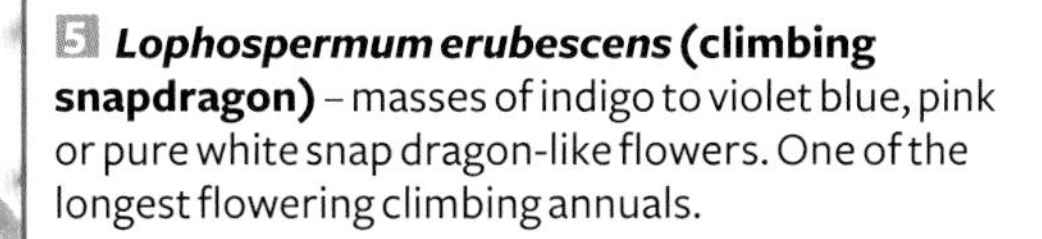

3 ***Rhodochiton atrosanguineus*** **(purple bell vine)** – fascinating pink and deep purple blooms. Highly recommended.

4 ***Eccremocarpus scaber*** **(Chilean glory flower)** – attractive leaves and orange or red tubular flowers.

5 ***Lophospermum erubescens*** **(climbing snapdragon)** – masses of indigo to violet blue, pink or pure white snap dragon-like flowers. One of the longest flowering climbing annuals.

6 ***Ipomoea purpurea*** – vigorous climber with striking purple, blue, pink or white blooms. Easily mixes with permanent perennial plantings.

7 ***Thunbergia alata*** **'Susie Mix' (black-eyed Susan)** – orange, yellow or white single blooms, most with very dark centres. Good for creating a tropical look.

PLANTING OUT

Gradually acclimatise young plants to outdoor conditions before planting in the ground, from May onwards when all threat of frost has passed. Annual climbers need a sunny, sheltered spot to thrive and they prefer rich, moist soils to poor thin ones.

If growing in a container, use a loam-based compost such as John Innes No2. Take action to prevent slugs and snails eating the tender young growth and feed with tomato fertiliser every other week when flower buds first appear.

Grow fruit in small spaces

April is a good time to shop for cane, bush and tree fruit. You should be able to pick up a bargain at specialist nurseries, as many will have knocked down the prices of old bare-root stock.

Even if you miss the bare-root planting window and can't wait until autumn, garden centres and nurseries will begin focusing their attention on container-grown fruit, which can be planted out at any time of year.

Many people are put off growing fruit – especially fruit trees – presuming that they need lots of space to grow. Not so. Most apples and many other tree fruits are available on special dwarfing rootstocks, which control the vigour of the tree so that they don't grow too big. And you can train them to grow flat against the wall of a house in pretty fan-shapes or grow them in large containers to create your own 'patio orchard'.

Most cane fruits (raspberries, blackberries and loganberries) can be trained along posts and wires – why not use this slimline display method along pathways or to divide sections of the garden up? – fruit blossom can be just as pretty as ornamental blossom.

Bush fruits like currants and gooseberries also don't take up much room.

Generally speaking, berries will crop in their second year, but you'll have to wait a few years before you can expect to see a reasonable crop of apples, pears, plums and cherries.

These 'investment' crops are well worth the wait, though –once trees are established, you'll be able to harvest tasty freshly picked fruit year after year, and make a significant saving on the supermarket bill.

For a quick fruity return, buy pot-grown strawberries from garden centres now and plant six in a growing bag – you'll be picking fruit in July.

THE DOS

- **Plant fruit trees in a sunny, sheltered position– pollinating bees will only visit to pollinate if the area is warm and not windy.**

- Opt for later flowering varieties if you're in a cold part of the country.

THE DON'TS

- Don't prune stone fruit trees (cherries, plums, nectarines) in winter – prune them now as they are coming into growth.
- **Don't plant fruit in a frost pocket: blossom can be browned and ruined.**
- Don't forget to check with your nursery or garden centre whether your chosen fruit tree needs a second (or third) pollinator nearby.

PATIO FRUIT

Fruit can successfully be grown in containers, but will need a little more pampering than if planted in the ground. Use a loam-based John Innes No3 compost and top-dress every spring with fresh compost and a slow-release fertiliser. Use a pot with a minimum diameter of 18in (45cm). Water and liquid feed with high-potash fertiliser regularly in summer.

TRAINED FRUIT

Cordons, fans, espaliers and step-overs are a brilliant way to grow fruit in a small garden. They look smart and take up little room. But there is an art to training and pruning them. If you want to get serious about this is style of fruit gardening, the RHS's *Growing Fruit* guide and Doc Hessayon's *The Fruit Garden* are an excellent place to start.

April

THE EDIBLE GARDEN

- OTHER JOBS TO DO THIS MONTH

SOW

- Kale, lettuce, hardy herbs and fennel (outdoors)
- Tomatoes (early April)
- Sweetcorn, courgette and melons (end of month)

PLANT

- You can still plant second early and maincrop spuds
- A new grapevine or fig
- Pot-grown globe artichokes and asparagus crowns
- Lettuces and herbs raised from seed undercover

GENERAL TASKS

- **Thin out** and transplant seedlings
- **Start to** harden off young plants before they're due to be planted outdoors
- **Earth up** potatoes once plants are about 6in (15cm) tall, covering the lower leaves
- **Hang pheromone traps** in apple and pear trees to protect fruit against codling moth
- **Provide support** for peas and beans sown earlier in the year
- **Look after the veg plot** – hoe and water regularly, and keep an eye out for pests
- **Feed currants and berries** with a general-purpose fertiliser

April project

Plant a container of herbs

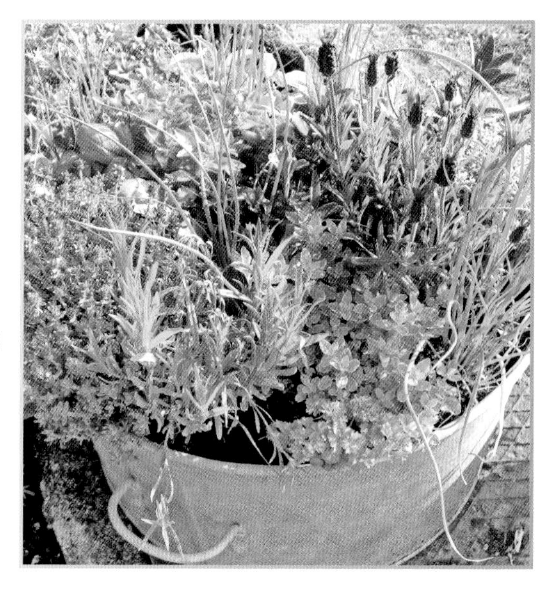

GROWING YOUR own herbs in a container by the back door to harvest when cooking makes sense.

Terracotta 'Long Tom' pots are ideal (three grouped together look attractive), as herbs love a long root run, but lower wicker baskets and galvanised tubs are fine, too.

Both annual and perennial herbs can be sown from seed anytime between February and August, but if you don't want the hassle of growing herbs from scratch, nurseries and garden centres generally sell young plants from spring; delay buying these until late spring, when the weather is warmer.

Sage, oregano and thyme are all useful herbs in the kitchen, and rosemary is another great addition, too. Always add some chives to your herb container – the sword-shaped leaves unite the rest of the planting.

TOP TIP

When cooking with annual herbs, always add the chopped leaves in the last few minutes so that they retain their flavour

Annual herbs like parsley, coriander and basil are summer essentials, and if you use a lot of these in cooking, it's a good idea to make extra sowings into small individual pots every three weeks to ensure a succession of crops through the summer. You can do this on a sunny windowsill and create a sort of 'production line'.

At the end of the season, your herb container will need to be moved somewhere frost-free and sheltered from wet weather. Woody herbs like sage, thyme and rosemary can be left in containers for several years, but to keep a plentiful supply of fresh growth each year, prune them back every spring.

If you're in a particularly cold region, then it's a good idea to take some 'insurance' cuttings during the summer in case your perennial herbs don't make it through the winter.

When to sow Herb seeds

- **Tender annual herbs such as dill, basil, coriander and tender perennial herbs such as French tarragon should be sown in spring undercover, and planted out when all risk of frost has passed.**
- Perennial herbs like mint, oregano, chives, thyme and sage should also be sown in spring under cover, or outdoors directly into the soil in May.
- **Seedlings and young plants will need to be nurtured in a light, warm environment until they can be planted out after all threat of frost has passed.**

PLANTING OUT

Use a container with drainage holes at the bottom and fill with a loam-based compost such as John Innes No2; mix in sharp grit to ensure the soil is free-draining. Depending on the varieties, you should be able to squeeze about six plants into a 12in (30cm) container. Place your container in full sun. Add a mulch topping of gravel.

CARE TIPS

Snip and tidy throughout summer to keep the new leaves coming. If there's a glut, cut and preserve your herbs by placing them somewhere warm to dry out; pick the leaves on sunny days around midday when the atmosphere is driest. Use labelled jam jars for basil, tarragon, oregano, sage and thyme. These herbs keep their flavour well. Water regularly and feed plants weekly with seaweed fertiliser during the growing season.

UNUSUAL HERBS

If you want to experiment with growing a wider, more exotic range of herbs, a good starting point is Jekka McVicar's *Jekka's Complete Herb Book*. It details over 350 varieties of herbs to grow and has over 200 delicious and inventive recipes. It is the herb-growing bible for herb enthusiasts.

VARIETIES TO TRY

Common sage (*Salvia officinalis*)
Eventually forms a large, woody plant. Will overwinter – cut back hard as the new growth appears in spring to prevent legginess. Take cuttings in early summer. 'Tricolor' and 'Purpurascens' are showier, though less tasty varieties.

Lemon thyme (*Thymus pulgeoides* 'Aureus')
Evergreen with small, bright yellow leaves that have a good strong lemon scent. Good for the front of your container. Trim lightly after flowering to maintain a bushy habit. Excellent in chicken and fish dishes.

Common chives (*Allium schoenoprasum*)
Cut them back hard after flowering for a fresh supply of leaves; divide in spring if necessary. Needs rich, moist soil. Mild flavour, good in salads and omelettes.

French tarragon (*Artemisia dracunculus*)
The best herb for chicken. Take cuttings as it hates wet winters. Do not confuse with Russian tarragon: the flavour of the latter is inferior.

***Mentha spicata* 'Moroccan mint'.**
Mint is best in a pot as it is invasive in the ground. Keep it in a frost-free greenhouse over winter. To revive it in the spring, remove from the pot, cut in half and turn the outside edges so that they face inwards. Top up with fresh compost.

***Rosmarinus officinalis* Prostratus**
Low growing variety, ideal for containers. Great winter cooking herb. Prune after flowering to encourage bushy growth. Take cuttings in late summer.

MAY

It's time to start hardening off tender bedding plants. You're usually safe to plant them out by the middle of the month in the south. Leave it until late May or early June north of the Midlands, and keep an eye on the weather forecast.

Earth up early potatoes if the shoots break through the soil, and pinch out side shoots on cordon tomatoes. Herbaceous plants will also be putting on lots of growth – support it with pea sticks or stake. Keep pests such as slugs and vine weevil (in pots) under control with biological controls that can be watered on, now that the soil is warmer.

MAY PLANTS 5 OF THE BEST

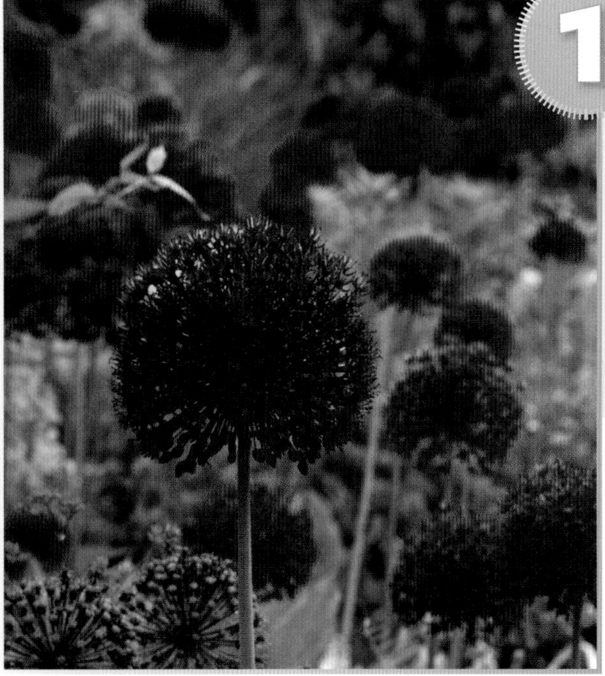

1 ALLIUM HOLLANDICUM 'PURPLE SENSATION'

Rich-purple lollipop flowerheads. Plant drifts of them through low-growing perennials for a striking effect. **H3ft (1m)**

2 CHOISYA X DEWITTEANA 'AZTEC PEARL'

A glossy shrub with elegant narrow foliage. Covered in white star-shaped flowers in spring and late summer. Bee-magnet. Tolerant of sun or shade. **H8ft (2.5m)**

3 BRUNNERA MACROPHYLLA 'JACK FROST'

A must-have for shady spring borders. Sprays of small blue flowers held about silver veined pale-green leaves. **H16in (40cm)**

4 DIGITALIS 'SUTTON'S APRICOT'

Gorgeous foxglove with soft-pink flowers in May-July. Hardy biennial – sow the seeds late spring for flowers the following year. Good next to purple flowers. **H4-5ft (1.2-1.5m)**

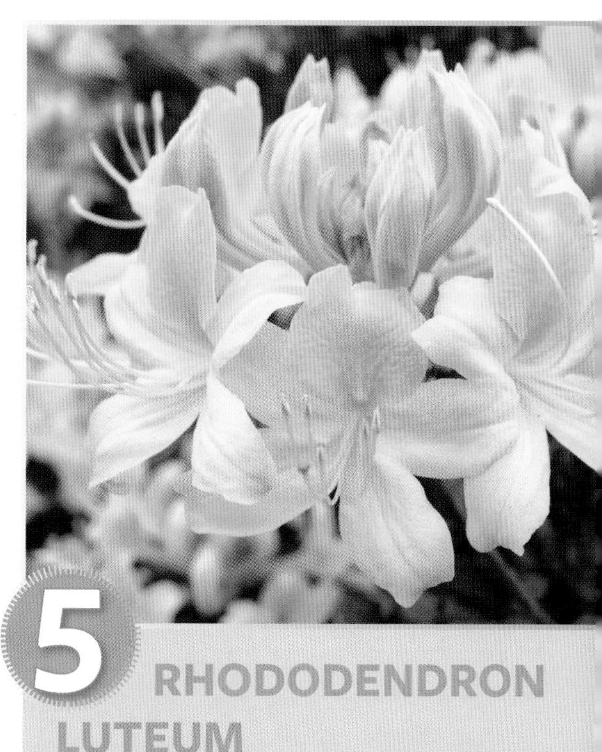

5 RHODODENDRON LUTEUM

A large deciduous shrub with beautifully scented lemon-yellow flowers. Good autumn colour. Needs acid soil. **H8-13ft (2.5-4m)**

OTHERS TO TRY

- *Enkianthus campanulatus*
- *Erysimum* 'Bowles's Mauve'
- *Geranium phaeum*
- *Papaver orientale* 'Cedric Morris'
- *Primula bulleyana*
- *Rhododendron* 'Blue Danube'
- *Tiarella cordifolia*
- *Wisteria* 'Amethyst'

MAY 2014

THURSDAY
1

FRIDAY
2

SATURDAY
3

SUNDAY
4

MONDAY
5

TUESDAY
6

WEDNESDAY
7

THURSDAY
8

AT A GLANCE
JOBS TO DO THIS MONTH

GENERAL TASKS

- ☐ Continue to hoe to keep weed seedlings down.
- ☐ Keep an eye out for pests and diseases – act quickly if you see any.
- ☐ Set beer traps for slugs.

PONDS

- ☐ Remove excess pond weeds.
- ☐ Feed fish regularly.
- ☐ Plant water lilies and other pond plants.

LAWNS

- ☐ Mow lawn weekly.
- ☐ Use lawn clippings to mulch borders.
- ☐ Feed the lawn in cold regions.

TREES, SHRUBS AND CLIMBERS

- ☐ Tie-in climbers.
- ☐ Trim evergreen hedging.
- ☐ Water newly planted trees and shrubs.

MAY 2014

FRIDAY
9

SATURDAY
10

SUNDAY
11

MONDAY
12

TUESDAY
13

WEDNESDAY
14

THURSDAY
15

FRIDAY
16

Remove excess pond weeds

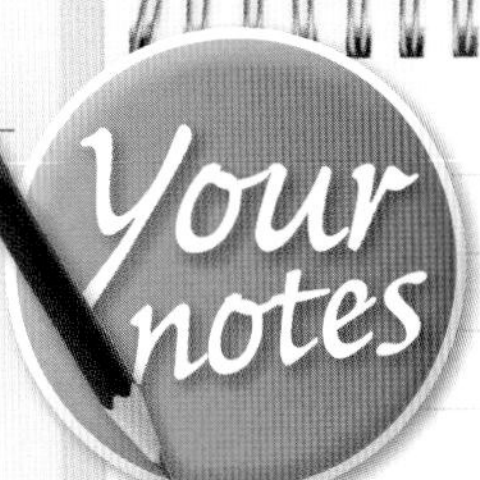

WEATHER:

PLANTS IN BLOOM:

TO DO:

MAY 2014

SATURDAY
17

SUNDAY
18

MONDAY
19

TUESDAY
20

WEDNESDAY
21

THURSDAY
22

FRIDAY
23

SATURDAY
24

AT A GLANCE
JOBS TO DO THIS MONTH

FLOWERS

- ☐ Plant out sweet pea plants.
- ☐ Thin hardy annual seedlings.
- ☐ Cut back pulmonarias and aubrietia.
- ☐ Feed spring-flowering bulbs.
- ☐ Clear out spring bedding.
- ☐ Plant out tender bedding and dahlias.
- ☐ Sow seed of perennials.

CONTAINERS & PATIOS

- ☐ Keep on top of watering pots and hanging baskets.
- ☐ Plant up summer containers .

IN THE GREENHOUSE

- ☐ Move conservatory plants outdoors.
- ☐ Take cuttings from tender geraniums and fuchsia between now and autumn.
- ☐ Shade glass and check temperature
- ☐ Bring out earlier planted hanging baskets or plant one up

WHAT TO PRUNE

- **Give early-flowering clematis a light prune if needed (pictured)**
- ***Kerria japonica***
- ***Spirea* 'Arguta'**
- **Forsythia**
- ***Ribes sanguineum***

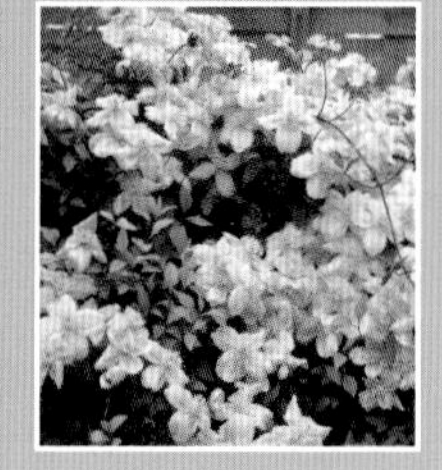

MAY 2014

SUNDAY
25

MONDAY
26

TUESDAY
27

WEDNESDAY
28

THURSDAY
29

FRIDAY
30

SATURDAY
31

Shade greenhouse and check temperature

WEATHER:

PLANTS IN BLOOM:

TO DO:

Control slugs and snails

We regularly list slugs and snails as our most-hated garden pests – and with good reason. They chomp their way through the leaves, stems, flowers and fruits of some of our most precious and highly prized garden plants.

Most at risk are the soft seedlings of bedding plants and vegetables, as well as young emerging growths of tougher plants, including delphiniums, lupins, dahlias and hostas. They also attack root crops and bulbs (they're particularly fond of tulips).

The tell-tale signs of slugs and snails are those slimy trails. This essential moisture has to be continuously replaced as they move about, which is why they thrive in wetter regions or after we've had rainfall. If you want to see how many you've got, go out after dusk on a damp, mild night with a torch – and be prepared to pick up dozens of them.

Because of the damage they do, and their propensity to breed by the hundred, they must be controlled if you are to have any chance of success with your gardening.

Here are seven top ways to do the deed:

Hand-picking

This does work. Aim to collect early morning or dusk when temperatures are cooler, as there will be more slug activity. Having picked up as many as you can, you'll then need to destroy them. Be ruthless – don't just throw them over the fence, as they'll be back! Either chuck them into a bucket of salty water or, if you have the stomach for it, snip them in half with your secteurs and leave them out for the birds.

Biological control

One of the most effective ways of dealing with the problem is to use a biological control in the form of nematodes in spring. Packs are available from garden centres, and from these packs you send away for the nematodes – a 'powder' that is then dissolved in water and applied to the soil. It is most effective when the soil temperature is above 5°C (40°F). The nematodes work by attacking the slugs and infecting them with a bacterial disease.

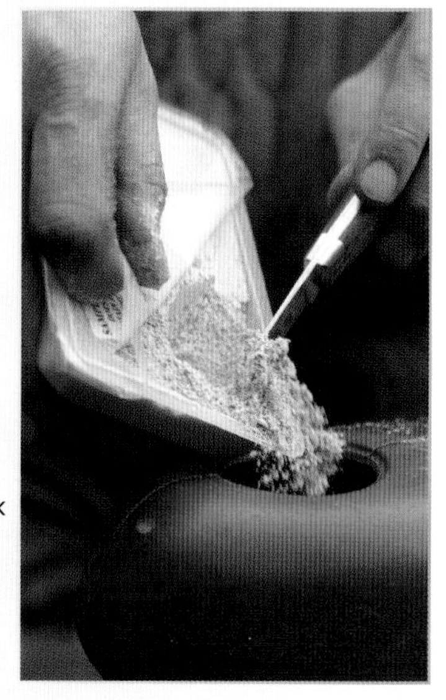

Slug pubs

This is one of the most popular methods. Filled with cheap beer, they attract the slimy pests from a few feet away. There are several 'slug pubs' available to buy, but you could have a go at making your own. Sink a plant pot saucer into the ground and create a 'roof' over it by placing an upturned sandwich box on four sticks to prevent rain diluting your bait.

Slug-proof plants

Yes, believe it or not there are many plants that slugs turn their antennas up at. For example, they hate hairy, aromatic and bitter plants so pulmonaria, lavender, and dandelions (shame!) are off the menu. They'll also give a wide berth to: hellebores, hardy geraniums and astrantia (pictured)...a little investigation as to which plants slugs avoid could change the way you garden!

Sacrificial plants

You could provide slugs and snails with more of what they do like! Plant a couple of succulent lettuces here and there in the flower borders to draw the slugs in, ensuring you regularly pick them off.

Attract predators

Birds, hedgehogs, frogs and toads all love slugs so make sure that you accomodate these natural predators as much as possible. Create a pond, plant trees, and allow hedgehogs access to the garden by cutting a hole at the bottom of a fence.

Pellets

Finally, we come to the least good method of control as far as the environment is concerned. It means spreading a poison, with a (slight) risk to wildlife, yet it is arguably the most effective way to kill the pest. Sprinkle a few pellets in the early evening, in damp, shady places where slugs are likely to gather, and around vulnerable plants. There are many different brands available.

Sow biennials for next year

Biennial flowering plants are brilliant for plugging the gap between the last of the spring bedding and early summer border plants.

They're sown from late May until late July, kept over winter, and then in the second year when the weather warms up, they're ready to flower and fill borders with early colour.

When you think about it, many of our most familiar spring and early summer border flowers are biennial in nature. Forget-me-nots, wallflowers and Canterbury bells (for spring colour), and sweet Williams and foxgloves (for early summer colour) are all biennials.

Sowing at this time gives the resulting seedlings time to mature into plants that will be tough enough to survive the winter.

TOP TIP
Once indoor-sown biennials have reached 2in (5cm) in height transplant them singly into 3in (7.5cm) pots of John Innes No2 compost

Sowing indoors

If you do not have a piece of spare ground to sow biennials outside, they can be sown into trays or pots and germinated indoors. Sow them thinly over the surface of the compost. Apart from the smallest seeds, you should either lightly cover them with more of the seed compost or a thin layer of vermiculite (which allows light and air to the seeds, without drying the compost's surface).

Sowing outside

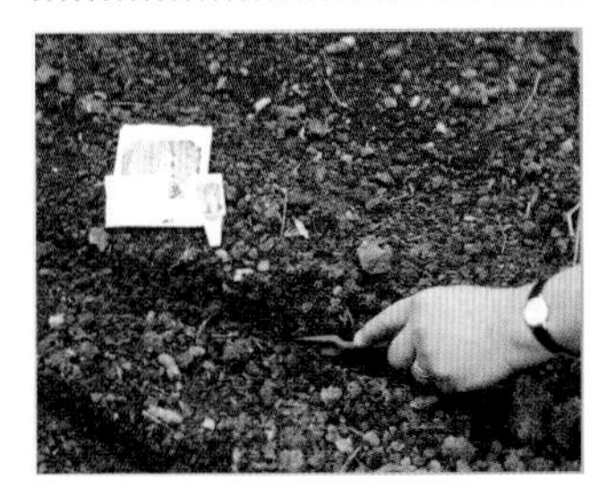

If you do have room in the garden for a 'nursery bed', first prepare the ground to form a fine tilth. Take out some seed drills 6-12in (15-30cm) apart. Then lightly water them. Sow the seed thinly along the drills. Carefully rake the soil back into the drill, and then firm with the back of the rake. There's no need to water again. Cover the area with netting if birds and/or cats are a nuisance.

Planting out

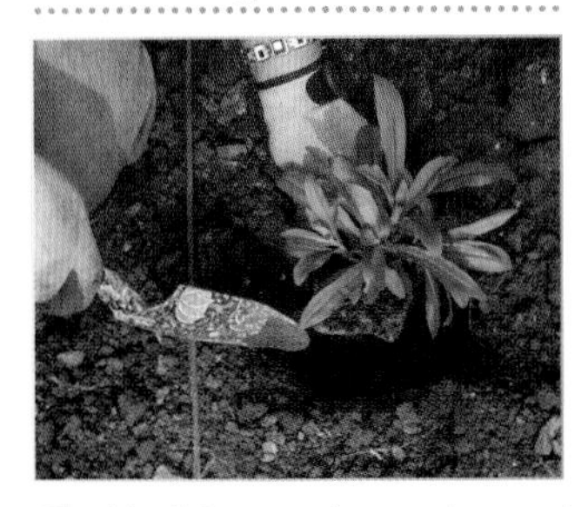

The ideal time to plant spring- and summer-flowering biennials into their final positions is autumn. Prepare the ground well and water in thoroughly.
Plant at the following distances apart for each variety: *Rudbeckia hirta* and East Lothian stocks 6-12in (15-30cm); sweet Williams 9-12in (23-30cm); foxgloves, hollyhocks and *Verbascum thapsus* – 18-24in (45-60cm).

WHAT TO SOW – 9 OF THE BEST BIENNIALS

1 CANTERBURY BELLS (*Campanula media*): Dwarf forms are suitable for rockeries, and all types are good for cutting.

2 WALLFLOWERS (*Erysimum cheiri*): Yellow and red are the favourite colours, but the range extends from creamy-white to dark crimson red.

3 FOXGLOVES (*Digitalis purpurea*): Usually seen in woodland gardens and herbaceous borders rather than flower beds, these can add height and interest to a late spring scheme.

4 HOLLYHOCKS (*Alcea rosea*): These can be grown as perennials, but rust disease usually attacks older plants, so it is best to grow them as biennials.

5 SWEET WILLIAMS (*Dianthus barbatus*): Densely-packed, flattened heads of sweet-smelling pink-like flowers in red, pink and white, and bi-colours of the three.

6 EAST LOTHIAN STOCKS (*Matthiola incana*): Double pink, magenta and mauve flowers, all highly scented, growing on stems 12in (30cm) high.

7 COMMON MULLEIN (*Verbascum thapsus*): Typically these have bright yellow flowers on spikes 6ft (2m) tall, with silvery, hairy leaf rosettes. Dwarf forms with darker shades, including pinks, are now available.

8 FORGET-ME-NOTS (*Myosotis sylvatica*): Dwarf varieties are suitable for edging beds and as underplanting for taller plants and tulips; flowers come in blue, pink and white.

9 RUDBECKIA (*Rudbeckia hirta*): One of the cone flowers, this is actually a short-lived perennial, but is best treated as a biennial; golden yellow daisy flowers with a black centre.

Grow your own strawberries

Strawberries are the quintessential taste of summer. They're straightforward to grow, once you get the hang of their three-year cycle.

In the first year, you'll get a small crop. In the second – and hopefully third year – the crop will be larger still, but after the third year they run out of oomph and need replacing.

Each plant throws out long stems, from which grow baby plants. These are called runners and need to be removed and replanted during the first year so that you always have second year crops on the go.

Traditionally, freshly-dug new strawberry plants are planted out in the autumn, but 'frozen' plants (cold-stored) and misted-tip plants (from cuttings) are now supplied during spring and summer. June to August is a good time to plant out, as plants will then have time to establish before cropping the following year. Remove any of the small white flowers that appear this year to allow the plant to concentrate on developing a good root system.

With thanks to Thompson & Morgan

TOP TIP
Don't plant strawberries near potatoes or tomatoes: they share a disease, verticillum wilt

It's vital that they are given a sunny sheltered site and go into good soil that's been enriched with organic matter like garden compost or well-rotted manure. The better the soil, the bigger the crop.

Tidy plants in late winter, removing any diseased or dead leaves – these could harbour pests and diseases. Protect early flowers from frost with horticultural fleece.

IN CONTAINERS

Strawberries can easily be grown in containers: fill with a good quality multi-purpose compost. Space plants 12in (30cm) apart. Position in full sun. Water in well. Keep an eye out for vine weevil.

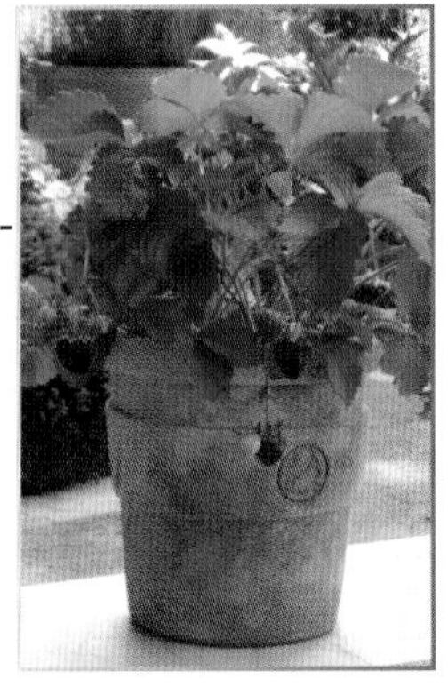

VARIETIES TO TRY

- **'Finesse' –** perpetual type with great flavour
- **'Christine' –** Very early-fruiting summer type
- **'Alice' –** mid-season summer type, sweet & juicy
- **'Cambridge Favourite' –** heavy flush of large fruits early and mid-summer
- **'Florence'** – late summer bearer

The essentials

1 PLANT OUT

Prepare the soil well by digging over and adding manure. Space plants 15-18in (37-45cm) apart, with the crown at soil level. Firm in and water well. Space rows 30in (75cm). Consider using a weed suppressant fabric to keep weeds at bay.

2 PROTECT

Mulch soil-grown plants with straw to rest developing fruits on. Pick off slugs and snails. Remove mouldy fruits and bin. Protect ripening fruit from birds with netting. Remove runners unless you plan to strike new plants.

3 FEED, HARVEST

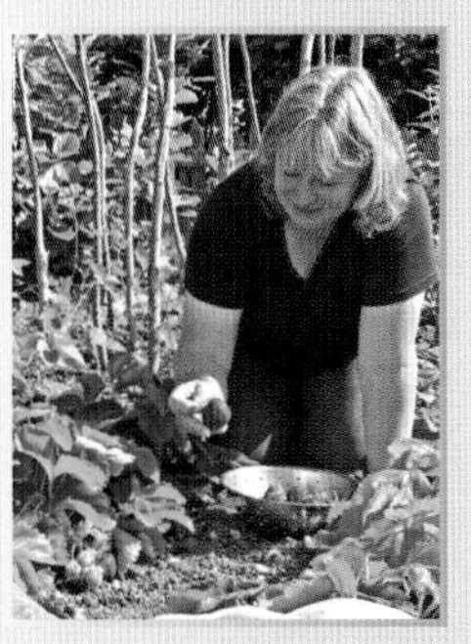

Water plants regularly. Give a high-potash feed from mid-spring, fortnightly until fruiting declines. Pick fruits as soon as they reach an even, deep-red colour. Remember to check plants daily as fruits ripen quickly in summer.

May

THE EDIBLE GARDEN
- OTHER JOBS TO DO THIS MONTH

SOW

- Runner and French beans; winter cabbages and spring cauliflowers

PLANT

- Leeks, tomatoes, peppers sweetcorn, courgettes, and brassicas (net them)

PRUNE

- Cut back hard the weakest shoots on summer raspberries

GENERAL TASKS

- **Pinch out** broad bean tips to prevent blackfly
- **Protect** young seedlings from late frosts

HOW TO PEG DOWN RUNNERS

Strawberry runners (long stems with baby plants at the end) can be 'pegged' into the ground – or in a pot of moist, gritty compost. When rooted, cut from the parent and either pot them up or plant in a new bed (never the same one) straightaway.

May project

Plant up a summer basket

PLANTING YOUR own hanging basket is so much more satisfying than buying one, not to mention considerably cheaper.

Yes, you could pay a tenner or less and get a decent-ish basket of petunias from the local market – but you want your hanging basket to be dripping with blooms and lush foliage. And if you plant your own, you'll not only have control of what plants go in, but the quality of the compost you use, too, which can make a big difference to displays.

Before you plant up your basket, make sure you have a good bracket in place. If you have an old one already there, check that it's still secure. If you need to put up a new bracket, hold the empty basket up to the wall to decide on the best height. Use long screws with rawl plugs, and only fix to a sound wall – a watered basket is a heavy item!

HOW MANY PLANTS WILL I NEED?

- A 12in (30cm) basket can hold one large central plant at the top, or three smaller plants, with a maximum of six plants around the sides.
- A 14in (35cm) basket can accommodate one large central plant and three smaller plants in the top. There should be a maximum of eight plants around the sides.
- For a really full, sumptuous look, go for a 16inch basket, and use 28-30 plug plants.

ESSENTIAL BASKET PLANTS

When it comes to hanging baskets, you've got to be bold – no half measures, so include plenty of pelargoniums, fuchsias, petunias and calibrachoa. But it's equally important to use several 'background' plants, like trailing foliage and small-flowered white and blue plants. These will help to bring the whole planting scheme together.

Lobelia 'Richardii'
This is actually a perennial lobelia but grow it as an annual and take cuttings from it in early summer to make new plants for next year. More drought-tolerant than annual varieties.

Lysimachia 'Aurea'
Trailing golden yellow foliage is good match for loud, bright flowers. For a softer-looking trailing plant go for silvery grey *Helichrysum petiolare*.

Sutera (bacopa) 'Snowflake'
This trailing plant is covered in tiny white flowers all summer long. Useful in any basket scheme to balance out other colours.

HOW TO PLANT
A SUMMER BASKET

1 You can use moss or special fabric to line baskets. A pre-formed liner can make life much easier. Some come with holes to poke the side plants through, but if your doesn't, carefully cut crosses with sharp scissors.

2 Part-line the base of the basket with a large square of thick polythene (such as from an old compost bag). Lay this on top of the fibre liner or moss. It will act as a reservoir and help to keep the compost damp.

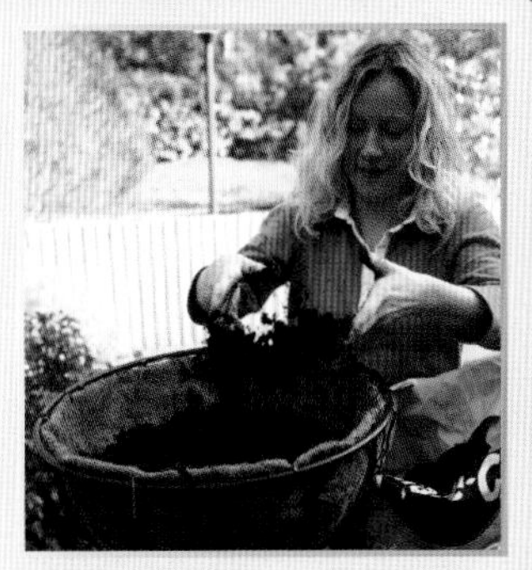

3 Now part-fill your basket with compost. Only fill to just below the side holes at this stage. Use the best quality compost you can afford. Mix in some water-retaining granules as you plant.

4 Decide which plants you want around the sides, taking their growth habit into consideration. Push the plants through from the outside, to avoid breaking any of the stems, flower buds or leaves.

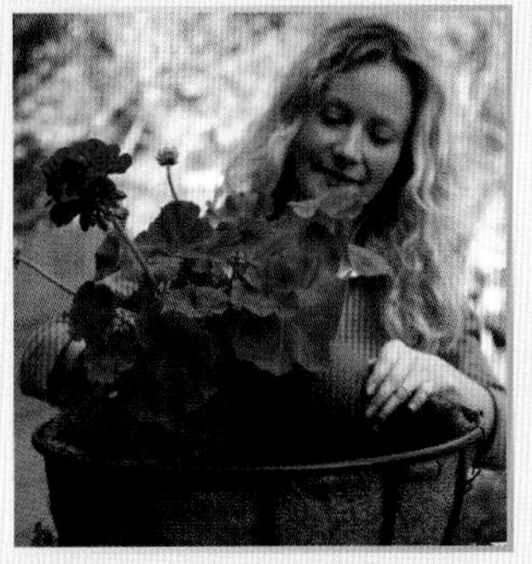

5 Add some more compost to the basket and then place a large plant in the centre. A bushy, upright plant like pelargonium or fuchsia will fill out the top of the basket nicely and avoid any unsightly bare patches.

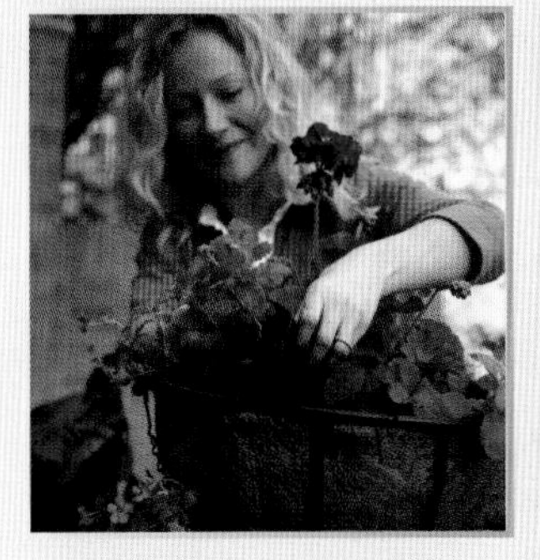

6 Now fill the basket with compost to an inch or so from the brim and get the rest of your plants in position. Water well, and keep the basket in a greenhouse to settle before hanging outside when all threat of frost has passed.

AFTERCARE

Once hanging baskets are on display, regularly water, feed and deadhead to ensure they stay fresh throughout summer. You may need to water every day during hot, dry spells; never water when the sun is fully out – do it in the morning and/or the evening instead. Add a dose of liquid high-potash feed to the watering can a couple of times a week.

JUNE

As the sun climbs higher it becomes stronger, so apply shading to greenhouse glass.

Start feeding tomatoes when the first truss of flowers appears – feed weekly and pinch out the lead shoot on cordons when the sixth truss has set.

Also feed summer bedding regularly, and deadhead often – this especially applies to sweet peas, which should also be tied to canes for support.

Deadhead repeat-flowering roses towards the end of the month. Leave once-only flowering roses alone to form hips for autumn interest.

Keep an eye out for pests on juicy young shoots and treat accordingly. Don't forget indoor plants, either, which will benefit from repotting and feeding.

JUNE PLANTS 5 OF THE BEST

1 CLEMATIS 'NELLY MOSER'

First-rate clematis suitable for sun or shade – the stripy pink blooms are stronger in colour when they are not bleached by the sun. **H9ft (3m)**

2 IRIS 'LANGPORT FLAME'

Bearded iris are one of the joys of early summer and there are hundreds of lovely varieties to choose from. Plant in bold drifts. **H30in (75cm)**

3 CAMPANULA LACTIFLORA 'PRITCHARD'S VARIETY'

Herbaceous perennial with tall stems bearing clusters of purple-blue bellflowers. A great companion for roses and irises. **H30in (75cm)**

4 EREMURUS 'CLEOPATRA'

The foxtail lily is a magnificent plant that soars above all else in the border. Needs full sun, free-draining soil and a cold winter to flower well. **H4½ft (1.5m)**

5 ROSA 'EGLANTYNE'

One of the best repeating English roses. Peach-pink blooms have a strong old-rose fragrance. Excellent compact garden shrub. **H3ft (1m)**

OTHERS TO TRY

- *Dianthus* 'Gran's Favourite'
- *Lupinus* 'Manhattan Lights'
- *Paeonia lactiflora* 'Sarah Bernhardt'
- *Syringa vulgaris* 'Madame Lemoine'

JUNE 2014

SUNDAY
1

MONDAY
2

TUESDAY
3

WEDNESDAY
4

THURSDAY
5

FRIDAY
6

SATURDAY
7

SUNDAY
8

AT A GLANCE
JOBS TO DO THIS MONTH

GENERAL TASKS

- ☐ Mow and tend lawns.
- ☐ Remove perennial weeds.
- ☐ Thin excessive growth of aquatic plants.
- ☐ Add tender pond plants.

TREES, SHRUBS AND CLIMBERS

- ☐ Clip box topiary.
- ☐ Deadhead camellias and rhododendrons.
- ☐ Take softwood cuttings of shrubs and roses.

FLOWERS

- ☐ Fill gaps in the border with bedding plants.
- ☐ Remove suckers from roses.
- ☐ Cut back oriental poppies.
- ☐ Harvest (and sow) ripe hellebore seed.
- ☐ Plant out canna and lily bulbs that were potted up earlier in the season.
- ☐ Plant borderline hardy ornamentals like agapanthus, salvia and penstemon.
- ☐ Plant out summer bedding.
- ☐ Take insurance cuttings from short-lived perennials like pinks (pictured).

JUNE 2014

MONDAY
9

TUESDAY
10

WEDNESDAY
11

THURSDAY
12

FRIDAY
13

SATURDAY
14

SUNDAY
15

MONDAY
16

Keep watering container plants

WEATHER:

PLANTS IN BLOOM:

TO DO:

JUNE 2014

TUESDAY
17

WEDNESDAY
18

THURSDAY
19

FRIDAY
20

SATURDAY
21

SUNDAY
22

MONDAY
23

TUESDAY
24

AT A GLANCE
JOBS TO DO THIS MONTH

IN THE GREENHOUSE

- ☐ Damp down greenhouse and apply shading.
- ☐ Control whitefly.
- ☐ Take cuttings of tender perennials such as fuchsias and pelargoniums.
- ☐ Water and feed plants regularly.
- ☐ Continue to pot up rooted cuttings and pot on young plants and seedlings.

CONTAINERS & PATIOS

- ☐ Plant up summer containers and hanging baskets, if you haven't already.
- ☐ Keep on top of watering and feeding containers and hanging baskets.
- ☐ Deadhead flowers.
- ☐ Bring out hanging baskets from undercover.

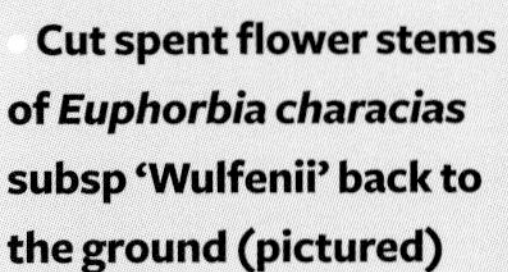

WHAT TO PRUNE

- **Cut spent flower stems of *Euphorbia characias* subsp 'Wulfenii' back to the ground (pictured)**
- **Deutzia**
- **Weigela**
- **Lilacs**
- **Trim privet and other fast-growing hedges**

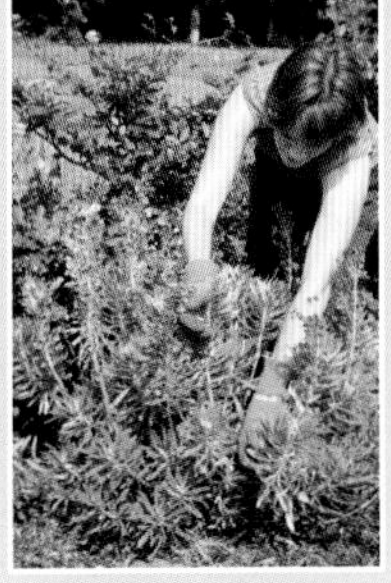

JUNE 2014

WEDNESDAY
25

THURSDAY
26

FRIDAY
27

SATURDAY
28

SUNDAY
29

MONDAY
30

Damp down the greenhouse in the mornings

WEATHER:

PLANTS IN BLOOM:

TO DO:

Plant a summer container

Long, warm, lazy days and mild cosseting nights – summer is a time when you can be adventurous with your containers.

Clement weather means pelargoniums can rub shoulders with South African daisies, and cigar flowers (*Cuphea ignea*) smoulder next to nicotianas. You'll need to keep on top of the watering though, but get this right and you'll be in for a real treat.

You can grow plants in just about any container as long as it's the right size and has drainage holes in the bottom. Taking the time to select the right shape, colour and material of pots for your style of garden will really enhance displays.

Choose a good quality compost, too, as this really can make the difference between healthy plants covered in blooms and a disappointing show. Peat-based mediums are difficult to re-wet; loam-based composts containing John Innes are a more sound option. Adding extra ingredients like grit and perlite is a good idea for plants that like very free-draining soil such as bulbs, succulents and herbs.

All will benefit from slow-release fertiliser being added in at planting up stage. This will act as a buffer if you don't keep up with liquid feeding later on. If you forget to add in granules at planting time, don't worry, make half a dozen holes in the compost with a pencil and add a few granules in each hole.

Step by step

The basic method for planting a container is the same regardless of pot size, compost or plants

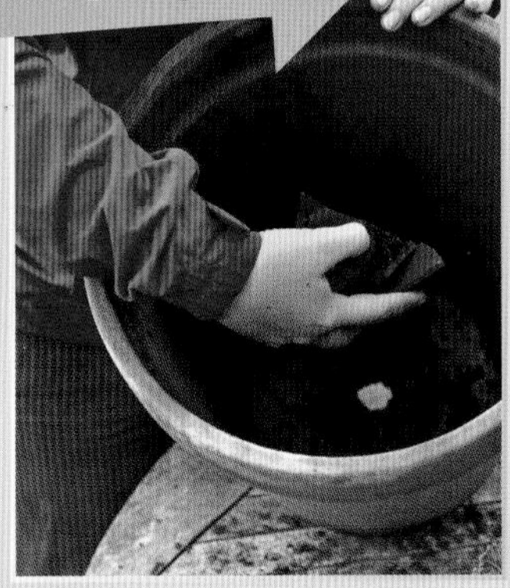

1 Ensure there are drainge holes in the bottom of your container. Cover these with bits of broken pots or pebbles to stop the compost from being washed out.

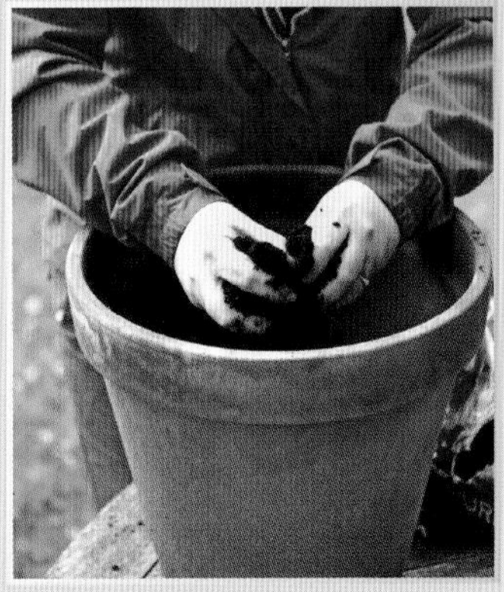

2 Start adding in your compost firming out any air pockets as you go; bump the pot gently on the ground to level out soil. Fill to about an inch from the top.

3 Arrange plants on top of compost, moving them about until you're happy with the look. Plant so the rootball tops are level with the surface of the compost.

THRILLERS, SPILLERS AND FILLERS

A fool-proof way to plant up a good looking container (large or small) is to stick to a simple recipe using three different types of plants – thrillers, spillers and fillers. Thrillers are taller showy plants that sit in the middle of the pots. Select these plants first then build around them with bushy plants – the fillers. Lastly add the spillers, which are planted at the pot's edge to cascade over the side.

ESSENTIAL CARE

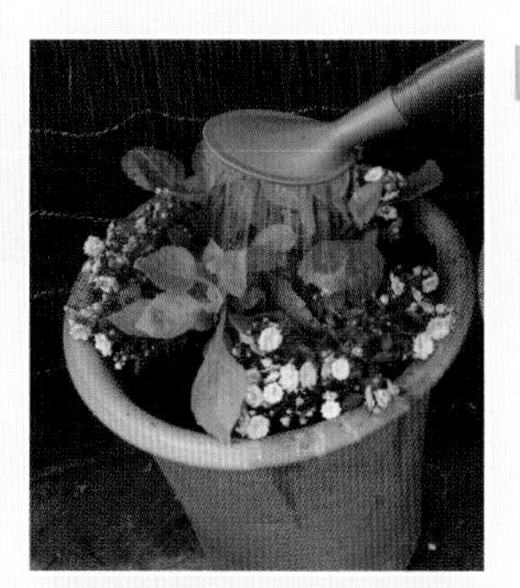

1 Watering & feeding

Never let container compost dry out. Add a dose of high-potash feed such as tomato or seaweed fertiliser to your watering can once or twice a week.

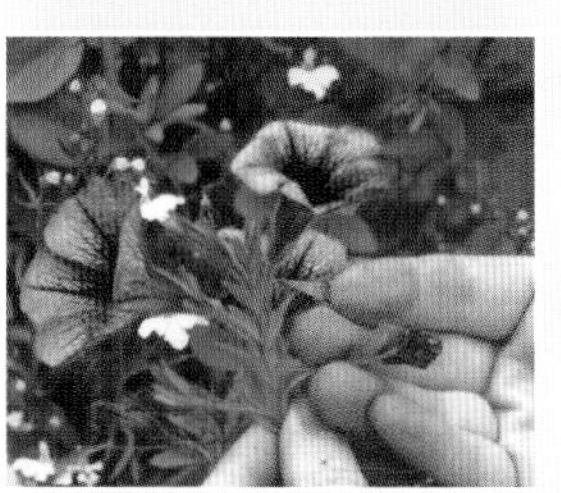

2 Deadhead

To prolong flowering and encourage further blooms, it is essential to remove dead flowers as and when they appear.

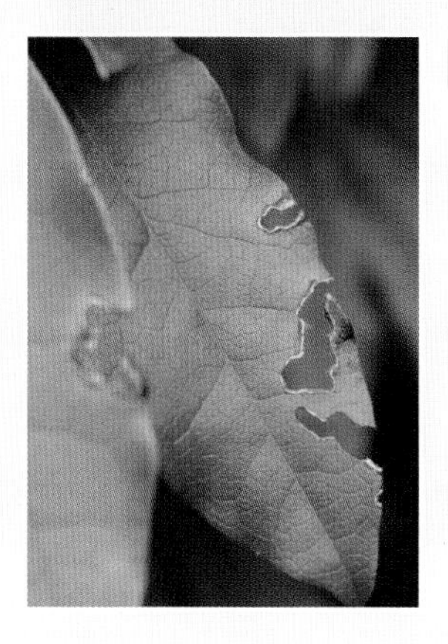

3 Pest watch

Vine weevil is the No1 pest enemy of pots. Look out for tell-tale notches on leaves. The grubs target the roots and the adults eat the leaves. Treat with a bio-control or spray with a suitable pesticide.

TOP PLANTS TO GROW

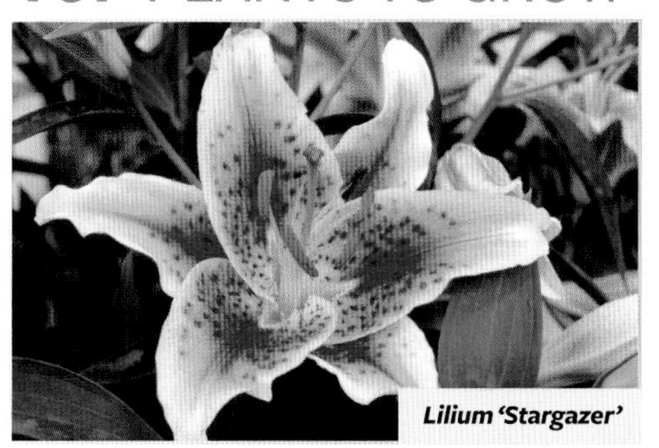

***Lilium* 'Stargazer'**

THRILLERS

- Asiatic lilies
- Argyranthemum
- Pennisetum
- Wallflowers
- Cordyline
- Pelargonium

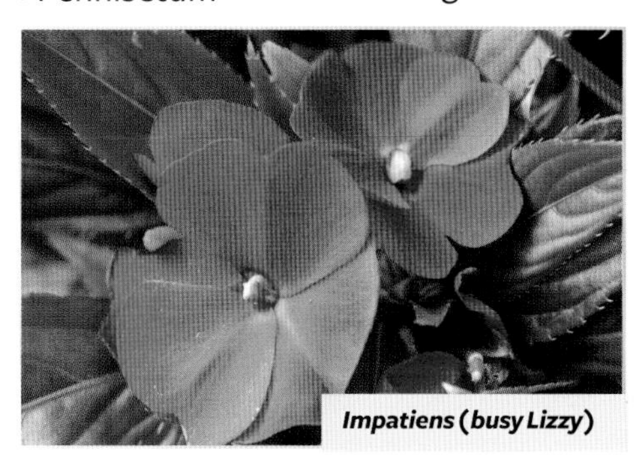

***Impatiens* (busy Lizzy)**

FILLERS

- Impatiens
- *Begonia semperflorens*
- Fuchsia
- Coleus
- Tagetes

***Carex trifida* 'Rekahou' *Sunrise*'**

SPILLERS

- *Ipomoea batatas*
- Ivy-leaved pelargoniums
- Million bells
- Carex grass
- *Helichrysum petiolare*
- *Sutera cordata* (bacopa)
- Trailing verbena

Grow your own runner beans

Runner beans are grown for their tasty, succulent pods, but they're also attractive climbing plants in their own right. Grow them up garden canes to add height and structure on the veg plot and enjoy the pretty white, red or pink blooms that precede the pods. They're not out of place twining up a rustic frame in the flower border, either.

Coming from Central America, this vigorous perennial is tender and should not be sown or planted outdoors until the end of May. Seeds can be sown undercover at the end of April for earlier crops.

Choose a warm, sheltered position for your beans. Dig over the soil and incorporate plenty of well-rotted manure – runner beans are hungry plants.

Plants will crop from June to October: pick regularly (once or twice weekly) for the most succulent beans. Pods left too long on the plant become stringy and fibrous. The fresh beans don't keep for long, so regard them as seasonal treat (rather like asparagus) and enjoy them during the summer months. If you find you have a surplus, they're easy enough to freeze. Top and tail beans and blanch them for a minute or two in boiling water before freezing.

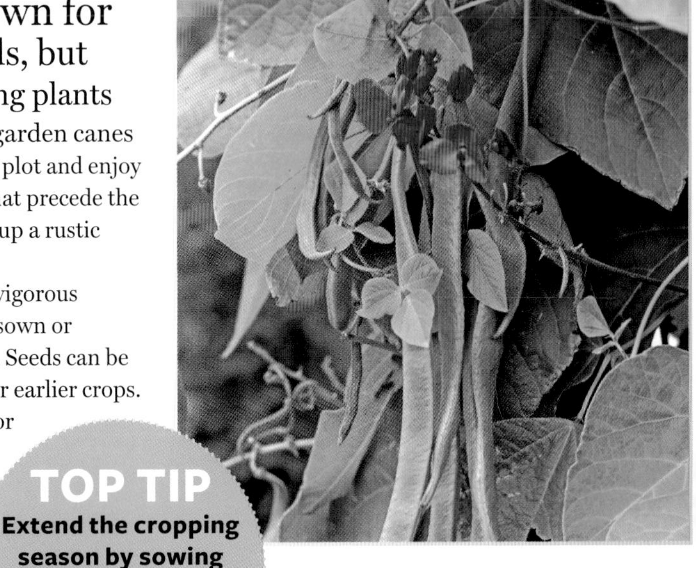

TOP TIP

Extend the cropping season by sowing seeds every four weeks from early April to late June

IN CONTAINERS

Dwarf runner beans are ideal if you don't have the space for climbing frames and can be grown in containers. The pods are tasty and full-sized but bear in mind they won't produce as big a crop as the climbing varieties. 'Hestia' reaches only 18in (45cm)

VARIETIES TO TRY

- **'Scarlet Emperor' –** traditional early variety. Full of flavour
- **'Enorma Elite' –** slim, stringless pods produced over a long period
- **'Moonlight' –** good flower set, even in poor weather
- **'St George' –** early and heavy cropping, with tender pods
- **'Painted Lady' –** good cropper with red and white bicoloured flowers

How to grow

1 SOW

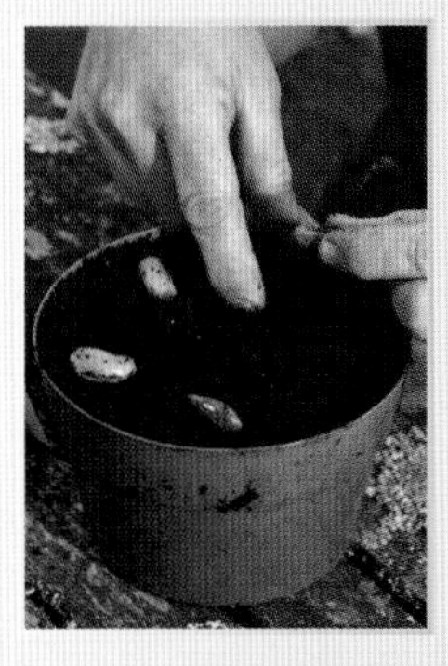

You can sow the seeds in pots undercover in late April and place in a propagator or sealed plastic bag, or straight into the ground from late May-early July. Grow the seedlings on in a greenhouse or on a windowsill and plant them out when frosts are over.

2 MAKE A FRAME

Use hazel sticks or bamboo canes. Form a wigwam or a traditional double row. Set poles approximately 12in (30cm) apart, and preferably position rows north-to-south, to get maximum sunshine on each side. Young stems may need tying to the canes initially.

3 PINCH OUT

Sow one bean or plant per cane, about 2in (5cm) deep. Sow a few extras at either end as spares. Pinch out growing tips when plants reach the top of the canes.

4 WATER

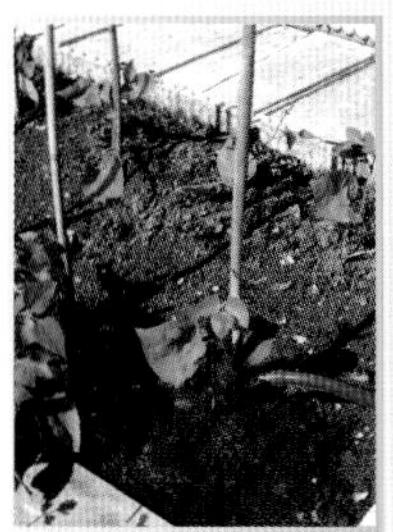

Runner beans are among the thirstiest of home-grown veg so water regularly, especially once pods start to form. Give the occasional liquid feed during the growing season. Hoe regularly to keep weeds at bay.

5 PEST WATCH

If black bean aphids appear on the undersides of the leaves, and the stems, spray with an organic insecticide. Watch out for slugs and snails, which are partial to seedlings and tender shoot tips.

June

THE EDIBLE GARDEN - OTHER JOBS TO DO THIS MONTH

SOW

- Sow Chinese cabbage and pak choi. Still time to sow carrots, annual herbs, beetroot, calabrese and peas

PLANT

- Tomatoes peppers, sweetcorn, cucumbers and aubergines outside
- Cauliflowers and greens

HARVEST

- Salads, broad beans, baby carrots and beetroot; herbs, asparagus, new potatoes

GENERAL TASKS

- **Watch out for** cabbage white butterfly on brassicas
- **Remove** strawberries infected with grey mould; destroy rather than compost
- **Regularly** water and feed crops in the ground, greenhouse and those in containers
- **Trim** and tidy perennial herbs such as sage
- **'June-drop'** is when apple trees naturally shed fruitlets; it is not cause for concern
- **Prune** the sideshoots of gooseberries and redcurrants back to five leaves

June project

Easy pond installation

PONDS ADD light and life to any garden. Once installed, even the tiniest of ponds will soon be teeming with wildlife, and any sunshine will make the surface glitter.

There are many different ways to construct a pond: from sunken concrete, raised brick and rubber-lined to shallow rain-fed pools and larger 'swimming ponds'. To look good, a pond needs to be in proportion to its surrounding area.

Hard and preformed ponds (that look a bit like jelly moulds) are a great place to start, as they're quick and easy to install. They can be bought off the shelf at most garden centres and depending on the size you've selected, you could install your new pond within a few hours. Preformed ponds need little maintenance once set in position and are long-lasting compared to their soft rubber-lined counterparts. Most offer internal planting shelves (different pond plants need to be planted at different depths) and some come with decorative preformed rock edging.

Site your pond in a sunny spot where you'll get the most enjoyment from it – you could even add a seating area nearby. Don't site too near trees or shrubs as leaves will fall in and rot, filling the pond with sludge that will foul the water.

TOP TIP
Ponds can be constructed any time of year, but early summer is the ideal time to add plants and fish

Step by step How to do it

1 Choose an open, sunny site away from areas of heavy leaf fall and sit your hard liner in place. Mark the soil around the edge with a garden cane, move liner out of the way and dig out the soil to the shape of the pond. Go slightly deeper to accomodate a base layer of protecting sand.

2 Remove large stones from the bottom of the hole and put in a layer of sand. Sit the liner in place. Use a spirit level to ensure everything is level – there's nothing more annoying than one end of the liner sticking up higher than the waterline once it's in place.

3 Fill with water. Filling up at this stage of the project will weigh the liner down and allow you to pack surrounding soil around it with little movement while you work. Tamp the backfill down firmly around the edge so that the soil won't sink down overtime. Make regular checks with the spirit level.

POND PLANTS TO TRY:

The following plants are suitable for planting into a large container or small pond (2ft/60cm diameter) and are available to buy online from **www.watersidenursery.co.uk**

1 ***Nymphaea*** **'Pygmaea Rubra' –** miniature pink waterlily with a plant spread of 18in (45cm). For slightly larger ponds go for a dwarf waterlily such as 'Perry's Baby Red'.

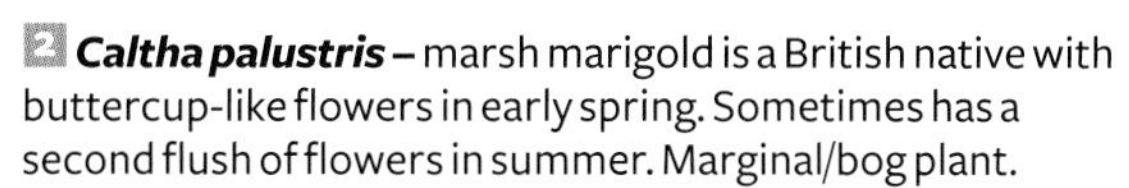

2 ***Caltha palustris*** **–** marsh marigold is a British native with buttercup-like flowers in early spring. Sometimes has a second flush of flowers in summer. Marginal/bog plant.

3 ***Iris louisiana*** **'Black Gamecock' –** bog plant/marginal with gorgeous dark purple flowers. Cut off spent blooms before seeds are formed. Divide every three years. Feed with fertiliser tabs or mulch well.

4 ***Potentilla palustris*** **–** scrambling, tooth-edged divided leaves and deep-red flowers in early summer. British native loved by bees and hoverflies. Marginal or bog plant.

5 ***Ceratophyllum demersum*** **–** hornwort is a British native. Is an excellent submerged oxygenator. Has dark green feathery foliage that floats freely.

6 ***Equisetum scirpoides*** **–** miniature evergreen marginal or bog plant with thin upright green stems with black rings. Does not require cutting back. Is not invasive.

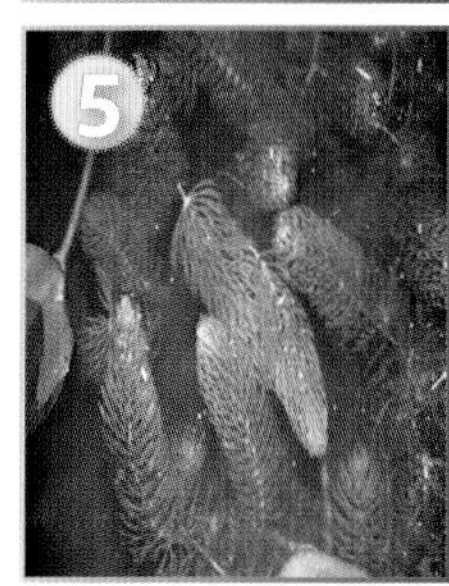

Pond plant images: Linda Smith/Waterside Nursery

4 Conceal edges with large flat stones or strips of turf, which will ppily grow right up to the water's ge. If children are likely to explore ur pond, consider cementing the ones in place to prevent accidents om occuring. Any gaps between or der the stones will provide hidey-les for wildlife.

5 Marginal plants (in their special aquatic baskets) can be placed straight on to the liner's shelf. Deep water aquatics – plants that need a depth of at least 8in (20cm) in order to grow well (most forms of waterlily come into this category) – need to be 'acclimatised' gradually to their eventual planting position and level.

6 Oxygenating plants are crucial to maintain a balance of oxygen in the water. They look good, and provide hiding places for fish. Sold as bunches of unrooted cuttings, with a weight at one end, simply drop them in to the pond. They will form roots and grow away happily with no further attention.

JULY

Midsummer, and if hot, dry weather persists raise the mower blades and cut less frequently; if the grass becomes parched don't waste water trying to keep it green – it'll soon come back to life when it rains again.

Continue to successionally sow carrots and lettuce, and take cuttings of pelargoniums, fuchsias and begonias, but keep everything shaded. Move houseplants outdoors, but do it in stages to avoid leaves becoming scorched. Also remember to keep weeds under control with a hoe in the flower and veg borders – but be careful not to damage the plants you want to keep.

After all that, make sure you sit back and enjoy the garden!

JULY PLANTS

5 OF THE BEST

1 HEMEROCALLIS 'FRANS HALS'

Beautiful bi-coloured daylily that flowers its socks off through July. Looks great planted with other 'hot-coloured' plants like cannas, kniphofia and crocosmia. **H4ft (1.2m)**

2 DELPHINIUM 'BLACK KNIGHT GROUP'

Dramatic spires of deep purple flowers above attractive, divided foliage. Cut back flower stems as soon as blooms are over for the chance of more blooms later on. **H5ft (1.5m)**

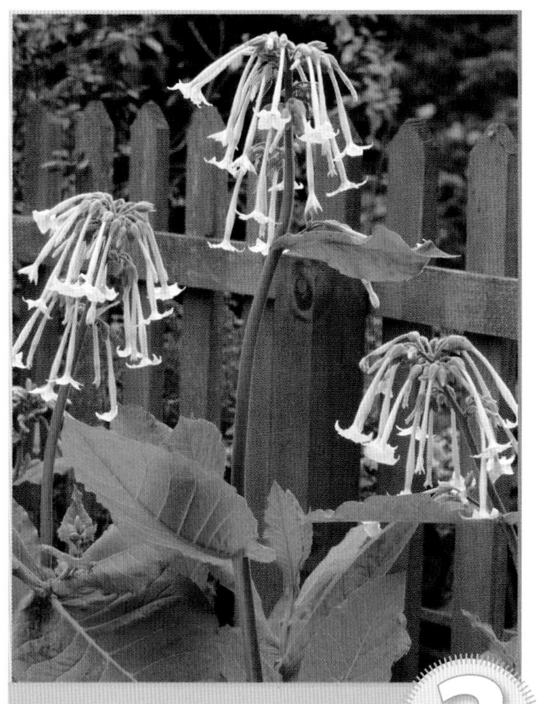

3 NICOTIANA SYLVESTRIS

Tall and stately tobacco plant with a fantastic evening scent. Use several as 'dot' plants throughout a sunny border. **H4-5ft (1.2-1.5m)**

4 COSMOS BIPINNATUS 'SENSATION SERIES'

Cosmos are a mid-summer must-have. They're easy to grow from seed, flower all summer long , and make great cut flowers. **H4ft (1.2m)**

5 TRACHELOSPERMUM JASMINOIDES

Be transported to the Mediterreanean with this fabulous jasmine-scented evergreen climber. It's slightly tender, so plant in a sunny, sheltered spot.

OTHERS TO TRY

- *Kniphofia* 'Tawny King'
- *Lavandula angustifolia* 'Hidcote'
- *Oenothera biennis*
- *Salvia nemorosa* 'Caradonna'

JULY 2014

TUESDAY
1

WEDNESDAY
2

THURSDAY
3

FRIDAY
4

SATURDAY
5

SUNDAY
6

MONDAY
7

TUESDAY
8

AT A GLANCE
JOBS TO DO THIS MONTH

GENERAL TASKS

- [ ] Ask a neighbour to come in and water/deadhead while you're on holiday – group pots together to make it easier; consider installing an automatic watering system.
- [ ] Keep on top of pests and diseases – warm weather will make them multiply rapidly.
- [ ] Top up ponds if levels drop.

TREES, SHRUBS AND CLIMBERS

- [ ] Continue to deadhead repeat-flowering roses; leave once-only roses to form hips.
- [ ] Sprinkle fertiliser around roses.
- [ ] Trim conifer hedges, privet and *Lonicera nitida*.
- [ ] Water newly planted trees, shrubs and climbers.
- [ ] Take softwood cuttings of shrubs.

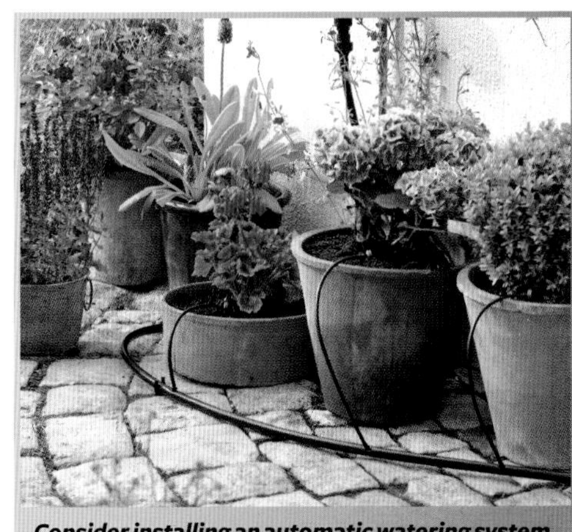

Consider installing an automatic watering system

JULY 2014

WEDNESDAY
9

THURSDAY
10

FRIDAY
11

SATURDAY
12

SUNDAY
13

MONDAY
14

TUESDAY
15

WEDNESDAY
16

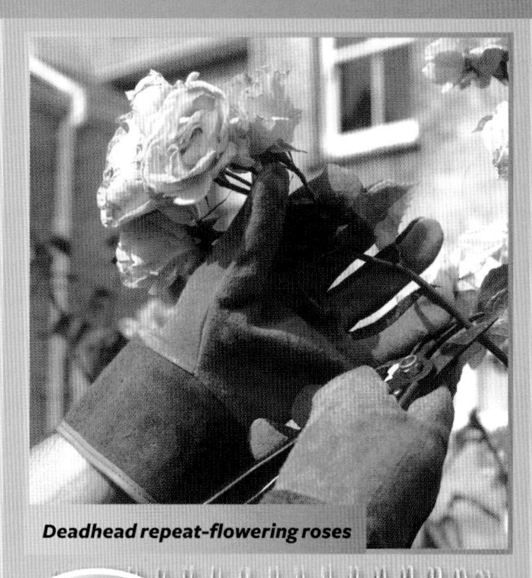

Deadhead repeat-flowering roses

Your notes

WEATHER:

PLANTS IN BLOOM:

TO DO:

JULY 2014

THURSDAY
17

FRIDAY
18

SATURDAY
19

SUNDAY
20

MONDAY
21

TUESDAY
22

WEDNESDAY
23

THURSDAY
24

AT A GLANCE
JOBS TO DO THIS MONTH

FLOWERS

- [ ] Water and feed herbaceous perennials.
- [ ] Divide bearded irises.
- [ ] Fill gaps in the border with bargain-basement summer bedding.
- [ ] Allow some plants to set seed, for collecting later.
- [ ] Cut back hardy geraniums.
- [ ] Deadhead, water and feed plants in pots and containers regularly.

IN THE GREENHOUSE

- [ ] Pick greenhouse crops regularly.
- [ ] Continue to sow biennial seeds.
- [ ] Keep greenhouse ventilated; apply more shading paint, if needed.
- [ ] Keep an eye out for pests – red spider mite, mealy bug, aphids and white fly.

WHAT TO PRUNE

- **Early-summer flowering shrubs such as weigela and flowering currant**
- **Clip lavenders once flowers have finished**
- **Trim back hedges**
- **Wisteria – cut back the whippy green shoots of the current year's growth to five or six leaves**

JULY 2014

FRIDAY
25

SATURDAY
26

SUNDAY
27

MONDAY
28

TUESDAY
29

WEDNESDAY
30

THURSDAY
31

WEATHER:

PLANTS IN BLOOM:

TO DO:

Lift and divide irises

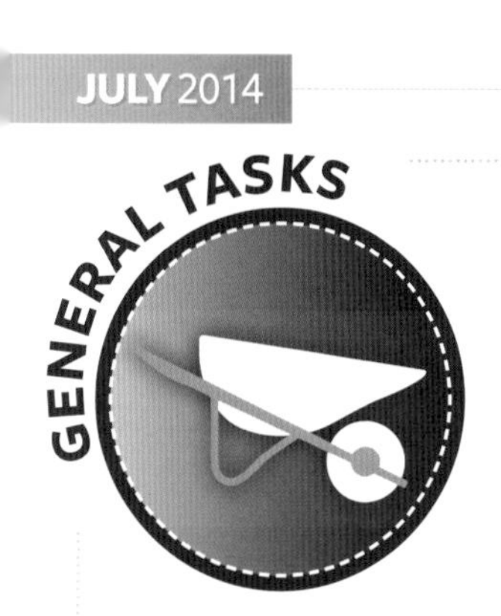

Take summer cuttings

Taking cuttings is an excellent way to get new plants from your existing ones, and will save you money in the long run. As well as increasing your existing stock, there are other good reasons to take cuttings: to replace short-lived perennials that have got too straggly, to produce exact replicas of the parent plants, and to create 'insurance' plants for borderline hardy specimens that might not make it through winter.

Summer cuttings are split into two groups: softwood cuttings and semi-ripe cuttings. A wide range of shrubs and perennials can be taken as softwood cuttings, using the tender new growth of the season. In theory, you can take softwood cuttings from spring through to late summer – but the earlier in the season you take them the better, as conditions are ideal and the aim is to get a good rootball to form before winter takes hold. If you do take them later in the season, make sure you can provide bottom heat for root formation.

Semi-ripe (or half-ripe) cuttings are normally taken in late summer when the stems have hardened a little. These take longer to root, and it may well be the following spring before they are ready to pot up. Often evergreen plants respond better to this style of cutting.

TOP TIP

If you can't find any non-flowering shoots to take cuttings from, do the next best thing – take your cuttings and pinch off the flowers

WHAT CUTTINGS CAN I TAKE?

SOFTWOOD CUTTINGS

- **Tender plants:** pelargonium, fuchsia, salvia, penstemon, osteospermum and coleus
- **Short-lived perennials:** pinks, erysimum
- **Perennial herbs:** sage, rosemary, thyme, lavender, hyssop and lemon verbena
- **Deciduous shrubs:** hibiscus, euphorbia, lavatera, hydrangea and buddleja
- **Others:** anthemis, aubrieta, gypsophila

SEMI-RIPE CUTTINGS

- **Most plants that take as softwood cuttings will also take as semi-ripe cuttings.** However the technique is more often applied to larger, hardier evergreen plants
- **Shrubs:** camellia, bay, erica, choisya and hebe
- **Climbers:** passionflower, solanum and trachelospermum
- **Perennial herbs:** if you missed the softwood window, these can be taken as semi-ripe

WHAT YOU'LL NEED

All you need is a few pots or a modular tray, clear polythene bags, a light, warm windowsill, and some gritty, free-draining compost. A half-and-half mix of perlite (or sand or grit) and cuttings compost is ideal.

How to take softwood and semi-ripe cuttings:

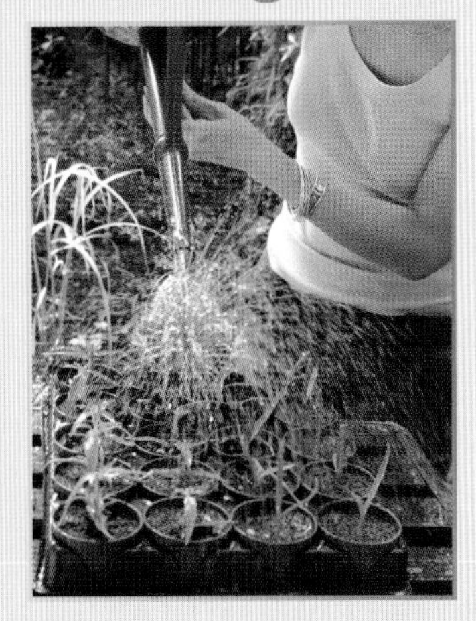

1 Water the plant you intend to take cuttings from the night before. With secateurs, remove 4-6in (10-15cm) lengths of non-flowering stem tips, cutting just above a leaf joint. Pull off lower leaves. Make a fresh cut just below a leaf joint.

2 Fill a modular tray or 5in (13cm) pot with compost. Make five small holes around the edge of the pot. Insert the cuttings and gently firm. Don't put cuttings from different plants into the same pot as they could root at different times. Label clearly.

3 Water them in thoroughly. Cover with a plastic bag or place in a propagator; remove covers twice a week to ventilate. If you aren't able to cover the cuttings, make sure you mist them often. Keep in a bright spot but out of direct sunlight.

4 Do not allow the compost to dry out. To see if the cuttings have rooted, check the bottoms of pots for the appearance of white roots through the drainage holes.

5 Once rooted (about 6-10 weeks later), pot up each cutting using a good quality free-draining compost and place in a sunny outdoor spot. At the end of summer, move into a coldframe (or frost-free greenhouse depending on the plant) for winter protection, until they can be planted out the following spring.

Grow your own artichokes

With thistle-like flowers and large, sculptured leaves that sparkle like silver granite, the perennial globe artichoke (*Cynara scolymus*) always puts on a dazzling summer show in the edible garden. Yet few gardeners have a clue how to use them in the kitchen, either leaving the flower buds too long before picking, or baulking at the fiddly preparation.

You can eat the young leaves (blanched), but usually we go for the fleshy parts of the flower buds that lie beneath the scaly skin – discarding the inedible bristly centre, known as the 'choke'.

The scaly buds look as impenetrable as an armadillo, but persevere and you'll discover that beneath its armour lies a deliciously rich, olive-oil flavour, with the texture of a ripe avocado. Two excellent varieties to try are 'Green Globe' and 'Violetta di Choggia'.

TOP TIP

When sown from a seed packet you'll get a mixed bunch of good, bad and ugly plants. Select the best and discard the rest

IN THE KITCHEN:

Prepare: Take a big bud and remove the roughest of the outer leaves. Place it on its side and slice off the top quarter of the leaves. Then cut off the stem from the bottom.

Cook: Place into hot water, add a few drops of lemon juice. Cover to keep heads below the surface. Simmer for 30 minutes, or until one of the central leaves pulls out from the heart. Turn the choke upside down to drain it and leave to cool.

Eat: The simplest way to eat a globe artichoke is to serve with melted butter or a mustardy vinagrette. Pluck the leaves and dip their bases into butter or dressing; scrape off the tender flesh between your teeth. Once these are gone, mop up the last of the dips with the heart. Alternatively, roast them, or add to salads and pizzas.

HOW TO GROW

1 SOW & PLANT

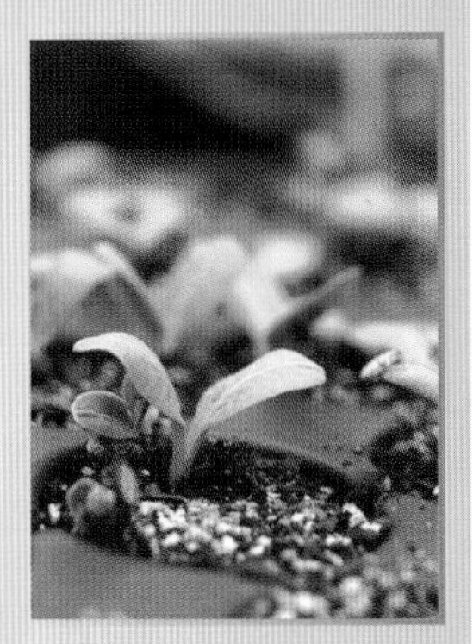

Choose a sunny spot with a well-drained soil. Sow seed in spring in shallow drills or in pots of good compost. Seedlings will need to be thinned – allow 2-3ft (60-90cm) between plants. Seed-grown plants usually flower the year of sowing.

2 WATER

Water plants well in dry weather. Blackfly can be a problem on young flower buds – spray with an organic insecticide. Weed around plants, and use a liquid feed following the first flush of flowers in summer.

3 HARVEST

Remove buds in July, just before the scales start to open. The younger they are when picked, the more tender they will be. If you want to enjoy the ornamental purple flowers, let a few of the buds grow on.

4 WINTER CARE

In exposed areas, or cold, northerly ones, tuck plants under a protective sheet of fleece during cold snaps when the temperature falls below 5°C (23°F). Mulch with compost or well-rotted manure in autumn.

July

THE EDIBLE GARDEN - OTHER JOBS TO DO THIS MONTH

SOW

- Autumn/winter salads, winter radish, spring cabbage
- Last chance to sow beetroot

PLANT

- Leeks, strawberries, endive salad and winter cabbage

HARVEST

- The first cucumbers
- Keep harvesting vegetables, don't let them grow too big and coarse
- Begin harvesting shallots onions and early potatoes
- Pick summer raspberries and cut back old canes
- Harvest blackcurrants, redcurrants and gooseberries

GENERAL TASKS

- **Water** runner beans regularly
- **Stop** climbing beans to encourage sideshoots lower down
- **Pinch out** the tops of tomatoes and beans, so they develop fruit rather than leaves
- **Prune** fruit trees that have been trained into cordons, espaliers, fans or step-overs
- **Cut back** old strawberry foliage after all fruit has been picked

July project

Grow holiday flowers

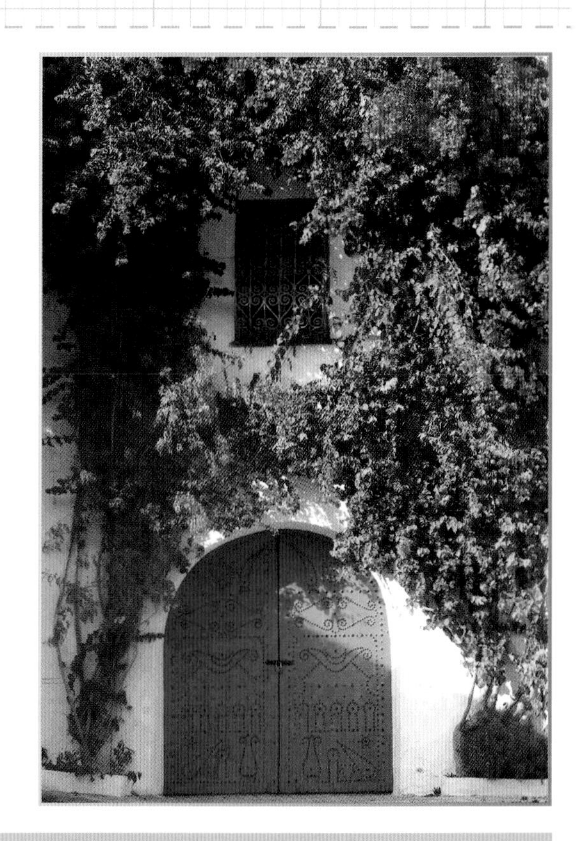

FOR GARDENERS, holidays abroad are doubly exciting because we can check out all the amazing plants growing at our destination. Luckily many foreign favourites can be bought in the UK. If you want memories that will last a lot longer than your tan, try growing the following plants from your favourite holidays...

NERIUM OLEANDER

In warm countries this evergreen shrub with flowers in either white, pink or red can reach epic proportions up to 6m (20ft) high. It's often planted as hedges – you might see them flashing past as you travel from an airport in Greece or Spain. In the UK, it's best to grow them in a heated greenhouse or conservatory, where a minimum of 7°C (45°F) is achievable. By all means stand plants outdoors for the summer, and if they grow too large, prune in spring.

JASMINE

The heady fragrance of jasmine will conjure sweet memories of your holiday for years to come. Europe is home to the common jasmine (*Jasminum officinale*) and its larger-flowered, pink-tinged form *J. officinale* f. *affine*. As you move south, expect to enjoy true evergreen Spanish or Catalonian jasmine (*J. grandiflorum* 'De Grasse'), whose flowers are widely used for the extraction of essential oils. In the UK, we can grow *J. officinale* outdoors and a hot, sunny summer will give the best blooms and fragrance. *J. polyanthum* is more profuse, but generally requires a cold greenhouse or conservatory.

BOUGAINVILLEA

Although native to South America, this showy climber calls to mind sunny breaks in places like Greece or Spain. There are many cultivars in colours of white, pinks, reds and oranges. The largest will climb to 12m (40ft) while others are small and bushy. All can be kept in check by restricting their roots to pots and pruning regularly in late winter or early spring. Grow them in a bright position indoors or in a greenhouse where temperatures will not dip below freezing.

POMEGRANATE

Although the pomegranate (*Punica granatum*) is native to what are now Iran and Iraq, it's often spotted on holidays in places such as Tunisia, Morocco and Egypt. If you have a sheltered site and well-drained soil it is possible to grow pomegranates outdoors here. The miniature version (*Punica granatum* var. *nana*) is easily cultivated in pots in a cool greenhouse or on a windowsill, and will still give you plenty of colourful (although tiny) fruits.

LANTANA

You'll see lantana in most warm countries, but it's a common sight in southern Spain. Flowers come in pretty colours of yellow, pink, white or tangerine. In the UK, lantana makes a pretty patio plant for summer, or you can keep it in a greenhouse (given a minimum of 7°C/45°F in winter). Unfortunately whitefly love it; but so do butterflies, which are attracted to its nectar-rich flowers.

CHINESE HIBISCUS

For some tropical splendour at home try Chinese hibiscus (*Hibiscus rosa-sinensis*). Its massive blooms, adorned by prominent central stamens, are popular with barmen in Caribbean hotels, who use them to garnish their cocktails. In Britain they make good houseplants. Position in good but not direct light, in a winter temperature of 10-16°C (50-65°F). With regular feeding they will thrive. Prune in spring if necessary and watch out for greenfly.

AUGUST

Hopefully you've been able to enjoy the fruits of your labours and have taken some time out to enjoy the weather. Greenhouse crops should be peaking now, so keep watering and feeding regularly, removing lower leaves from tomato plants to focus their efforts on the fruit. It's not too late to summer-prune apples; also prune raspberry canes after fruiting.

Keep an eye out for powdery mildew on sweet peas and courgettes if the weather's hot and dry; mulching plants straight after a good drenching of water will help.

Flower borders can look lacklustre during August – for an instant colour boost plug gaps with late-summer flowering perennials like penstemons, dahlias and rudbeckia.

AUGUST PLANTS

5 OF THE BEST

1 EUCOMIS BICOLOR

Spectacular exotic-looking summer bulb. Not hardy in frost-prone areas, so grow in a pot and overwinter in a cool greenhouse. **H2ft (60cm)**

2 CANNA 'PHASION' (SYN TROPICANNA)

Grown for its striking purple, orange and green striped foliage and bright orange flowers. Good in a 'hot-themed' planting scheme. **H5ft (1.5m)**

3 OSTEOSPERMUM JACUNDUM

One of the hardier cape daisies, but ensure it's planted in free-draining soil and in full sun. Smothered with pink daisy flowers all summer.
H19in (48cm)

4 AGAPANTHUS 'LOCH HOPE'

Late flowering variety with deep-blue trumpet-shaped flowers. Is hardy but mulch before winter in cold areas **4ft (1.2m)**

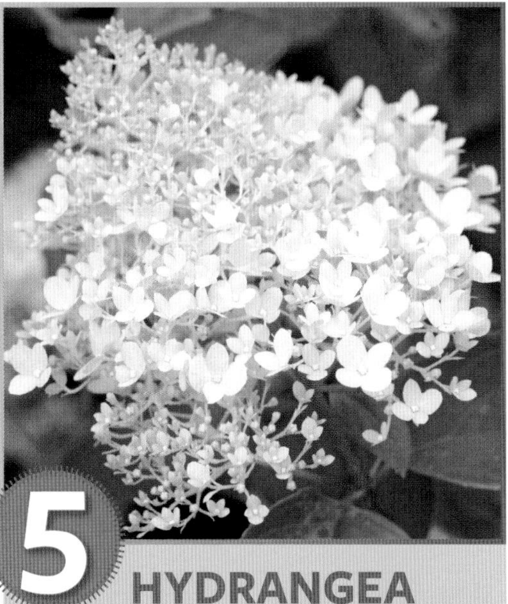

5 HYDRANGEA PANICULATA 'LIMELIGHT'

Dramatic hydrangea with conical ivory-white flowerheads that flush pink as they age. **8ft (2.4m)**

OTHERS TO TRY

- *Buddleja davidii* 'Black Knight'
- *Cosmos atrosanguineus*
- *Helenium* 'Sahin's Early Flowerer'
- *Lonicera periclymenum* 'Serotina'

AUGUST 2014

FRIDAY
1

SATURDAY
2

SUNDAY
3

MONDAY
4

TUESDAY
5

WEDNESDAY
6

THURSDAY
7

FRIDAY
8

AT A GLANCE
JOBS TO DO THIS MONTH

GENERAL TASKS

- ☐ Watch out for powdery mildew on honeysuckle and roses.
- ☐ Keep an eye out for slugs in cool, wet weather; apply slug controls.
- ☐ Keep plants well watered and fed, particularly those in containers.
- ☐ Deadhead flowers to stop seed setting and encourage more blooms.
- ☐ Control vine weevil in containers.
- ☐ Mow lawns, but don't feed or water.
- ☐ Clear out yellow or decomposing water lily leaves from ponds.
- ☐ Top up ponds (ideally with rainwater), especially if you're going on holiday.

TREES, SHRUBS AND CLIMBERS

- ☐ Trim hedges like hornbeam, Leyland cypress, beech and thuja.
- ☐ Feed camellias and rhododendrons and water well.
- ☐ Take semi-ripe cuttings of herbs.
- ☐ Propagate clematis by layering.

Control vine veevil in containers

AUGUST 2014

SATURDAY
9

SUNDAY
10

MONDAY
11

TUESDAY
12

WEDNESDAY
13

THURSDAY
14

FRIDAY
15

SATURDAY
16

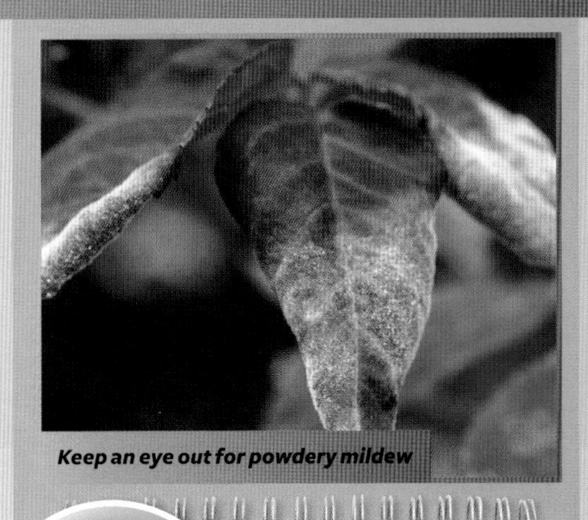

Keep an eye out for powdery mildew

Your notes

WEATHER:

PLANTS IN BLOOM:

TO DO:

AUGUST 2014

SUNDAY
17

MONDAY
18

TUESDAY
19

WEDNESDAY
20

THURSDAY
21

FRIDAY
22

SATURDAY
23

SUNDAY
24

AT A GLANCE
JOBS TO DO THIS MONTH

FLOWERS

- ☐ Set earwig traps around chrysanths and dahlias.
- ☐ Trim back perennials that have flopped over.
- ☐ Save seed from hardy annuals perennials and bulbs.
- ☐ Pot up self-sown seedlings.
- ☐ Plant autumn-flowering bulbs.
- ☐ Take cuttings of alpines.

IN THE GREENHOUSE

- ☐ Ventilate greenhouse regularly.
- ☐ Traditional month for taking cuttings of pelargoniums and fuchsias.
- ☐ You can start potting up hyacinths for Christmas flowers (see pp146-147).

CONTAINERS & PATIOS

- ☐ Keep watering and feeding containers and hanging baskets.

WHAT TO PRUNE

- **Rambling roses**
- **Trim lavender, rosemary and santolina**
- **Finish summer pruning of wisteria**

AUGUST 2014

MONDAY
25

TUESDAY
26

WEDNESDAY
27

THURSDAY
28

FRIDAY
29

SATURDAY
30

SUNDAY
31

Trap earwigs in upturned pots stuffed with straw

Your notes

WEATHER:

PLANTS IN BLOOM:

TO DO:

Take pelargonium cuttings

From single flowers to semi-doubles, and from scented leaves to trailing forms, there are hundreds of pelargoniums (commonly known as tender geraniums) to choose from. Every summer garden should have a couple of different forms of tender geranium: they'll repay you with continuity of flower from May until the first frosts of autumn.

A large pelargonium in flower from the garden centre can be costly. Cheaper but smaller plants bought in strips in spring are available, but by the time they've reached a good size, the season's well underway.

If you want large plants at little cost for the start of the next year's season, take cuttings in August from the current year's plants. You can in fact take cuttings as late as October, but if you start them in August you can revisit the parent plants several times.

TOP TIP

Don't be disheartened if you lose some of your cuttings to grey mould disease – even professional growers don't achieve a 100% success rate

TIPS ON TAKING CUTTINGS

- **Always take more cuttings than you need – there are bound to be a few casualties.**
- Make sure compost is free-draining – a mix of 50 per cent grit and 50 per cent cuttings compost.
- **Remove all lower leaves – if there are too many leaves, cuttings will lose moisture, wilt and die.**
- Place cuttings somewhere frost-free and slightly shaded. Keep compost on the dryish side but don't let it dry out completely.
- **Ensure there is good air circulation around cuttings. Don't cover with plastic bags – moisture inside the bags may cause them to rot.**

Did you know?

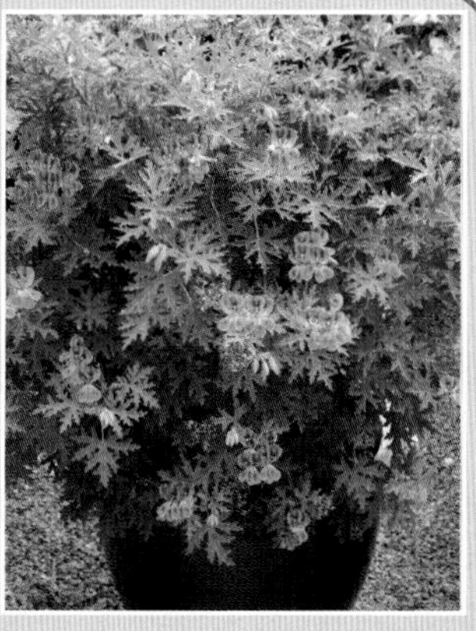

You can keep your pelargoniums producing flowers right up until Christmas? Move them to a sunny windowsill indoors. Keep lightly watered, deadhead, and give a regular feed of potash fertiliser. Re-pot in the spring before planting out again. Plants can be overwintered like this for several years, but they will become woody in time and need replacing.

HOW TO TAKE CUTTINGS

• **The best cuttings material comes from ripe, non-flowering growing shoots,** Cut just above the leaf joint when it is taken from the plant. Ensure shoots are not too plump, however, as these are more prone to rotting.

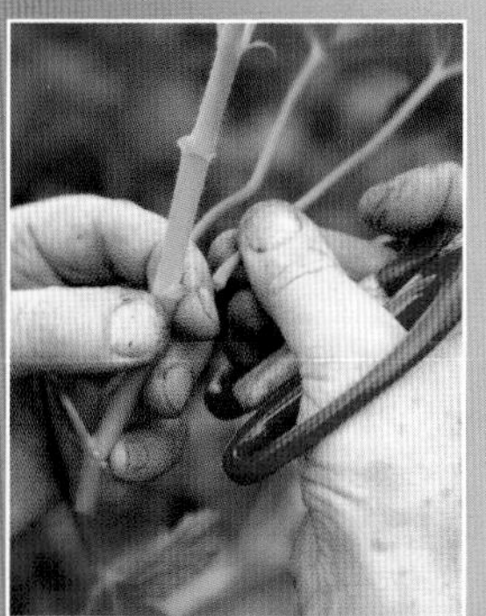

• **Carefully remove all the lower leaves,** but leave two or three at the top of the cutting. Hold shoots at their joints and pull off the leaf stalks in an upwards movement to create a larger surface area for roots to form.

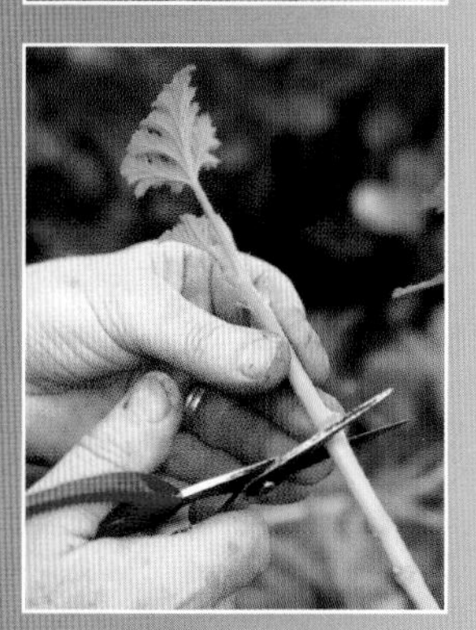

• **Once the leaves are off, trim the cutting to just below a joint.** The length of the cutting should be about 3-4in (7.5-10cm). Mix a good quality seed compost with horticultural grit (50 per cent of each) and fill a modular tray with it.

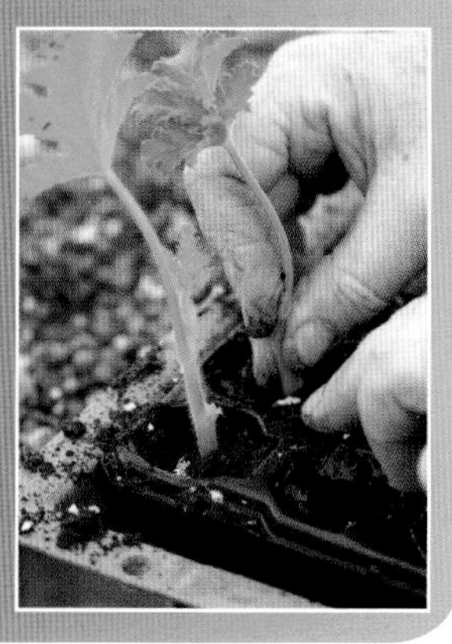

• **Push cuttings into the compost and label them.** Keep them somewhere slightly shaded, and airy. Most importantly, keep the plants frost-free over winter, and pot each rooted cutting up once in late winter or early spring, before hardening them off.

FIVE PELARGONIUMS TO GROW

With thanks to Fibrex Nurseries/ www.fibrex.co.uk

1 'Lord Bute'
Dramatic black-purple blooms – one of the best regal pelargoniums

2 'Choun Cho'
Trailing, ivy-leaved, maroon flowers – a favourite at Windsor Castle

3 'Ardens'
Gorgeous small blood-red flowers, looks striking in a terracotta pot

4 'Grey Lady Plymouth'
Delightful mint-scented finely divided leaves. Well-loved by pelargonium connoisseurs

5 'Tornado'
Neat and compact with large flowers, excellent in window boxes or hanging baskets

Tomato problems

Regardless of the fact that a lot of us grow tomatoes every year, the truth of the matter is that the British climate is usually far from ideal for them. This causes the plants – and fruits – to be susceptible to a few pests and diseases. But don't let this put you off growing them – tomato problems are rarely fatal and are easily dealt with if they are spotted early enough.

Just by looking at the leaves you can usually tell a healthy tomato plant from an unhealthy one – the foliage is often the first thing to reveal a problem. For instance, sometimes the leaves curl up. This is probably just a shortage of water at the roots – tomatoes are thirsty plants – and a good soaking will restore the leaves to their usual shape in a few hours. But it may be a sign that something more serious is wrong, like the fungal disease blight, which has become a big problem in recent years with all the damp summers we've been experiencing.

Here is a round-up of the most common tomato problems, along with advice on what to do if disease – or anything else – threatens your crop.

5 CULTURAL PROBLEMS

The following problems are all brought about as a result of environmental conditions, or by things the gardener has – or hasn't – done to the plants.

Blossom end rot

Sunken dark brown areas form at the base of swelling tomato fruits. This is caused by a lack of calcium in the plant, a result of interrupted uptake of moisture (erratic watering).
It can be remedied by more even and efficient watering – several times a day if required.

Greenback

A green or yellow ring of unripened tissue remains around the stalk end of the tomato. Combat by improving ventilation and shade. Weekly feeds of a tomato fertiliser will help. Or try resistant varieties such as 'Moneymaker' and 'Alicante'.

Splitting

Fruits develop normally and then, frequently just before we want to pick them, they split open. This is caused by erratic swelling of the fruit. Keep the compost moist, and in the greenhouse try to improve ventilation. Affected fruits can still be used in cooking.

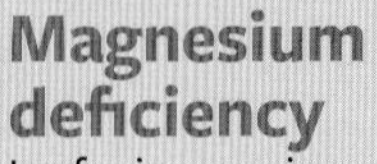

Leaf veins remain green but the areas between them go yellow. Eventually leaves die and fall off. Over-use of potash feed can be the culprit. To remedy the problem, apply Epsom salts as a foliar feed.

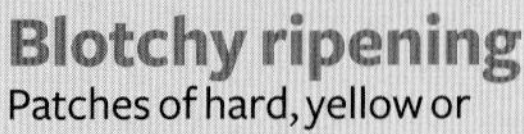

Patches of hard, yellow or green flesh remain unripened. Probably indicates potassium deficiency. Dry soil or compost and high temperature can be factors. Keep plants well fed and watered and the greenhouse well ventilated.

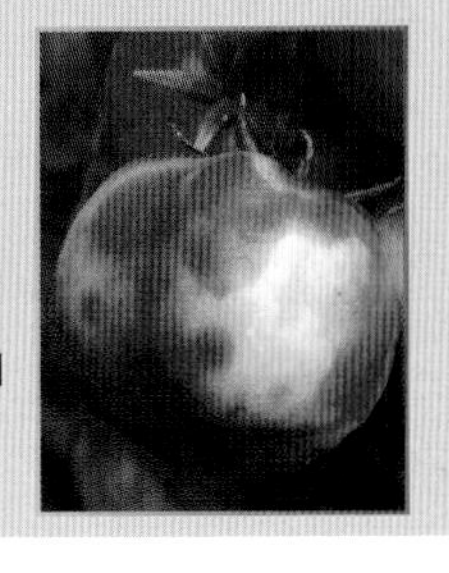

3 TOMATO PESTS

Whitefly

Heavy infestations of whitefly can severely weaken plants. Plant French marigolds (to deter the pest) nearby; in the greenhouse you could introduce the encarsia wasp – a biological control. Or spray with a insectide for fruit and veg.

Red spider mite

This pest is only problematic with greenhouse-grown tomato crops. Tiny mites spin webbing in leaf crevices. They can suck the life out of a tomato plant. Biological control is available in the form of the phytoseiulus predator, or spray with an approved insecticide.

Tomato moth

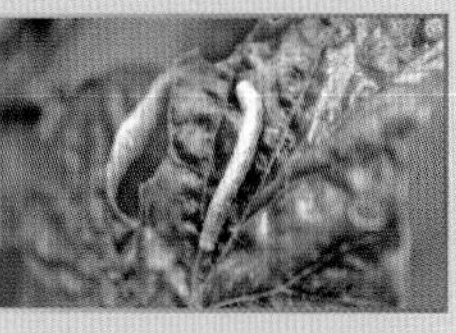

Both the leaves and the fruits are eaten by green caterpillars that can reach up to an inch long. They are easily picked off and dispose of, or in severe infestations you can spray the caterpillars with an approved bug killer.

2 TOMATO DISEASES

Tomato blight

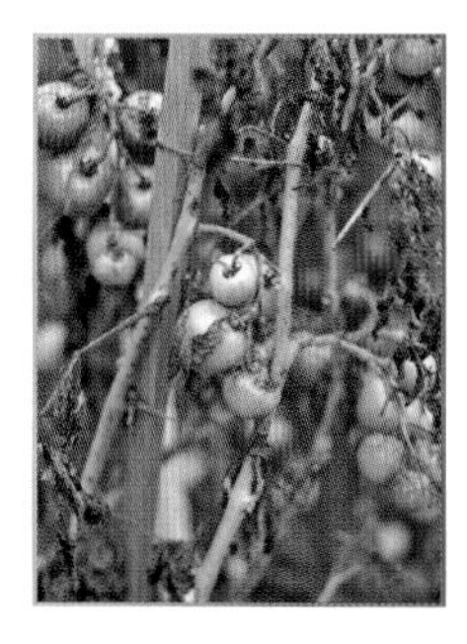

The most serious tomato disease: an airborne fungus that easily spreads in warm, wet weather. Stems, leaves and fruits wither and die. Destroy infected plants. Grow undercover rather than in the open. Go for early-to-mature varieties.

Ghost spot

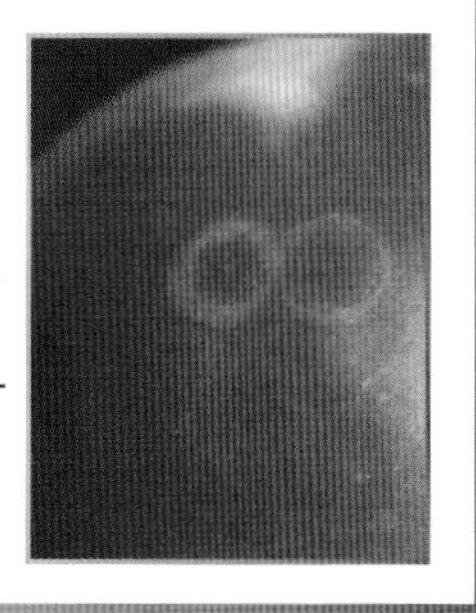

Pale rings appear on the skins of tomato fruits. Cause: *Botrytis cinerea* fungus. The fruit's development is not hindered and it can still be eaten. This widespread fungus is difficult to control. Rotate your crops next year.

August

THE EDIBLE GARDEN - OTHER JOBS TO DO THIS MONTH

SOW

- Last sowing of fast-maturing carrot like 'Early Nantes'. Also winter-hardy spring onions.
- Rocket and sugarloaf chicory

PLANT

- Hardy winter crops like spring cauliflowers and sprouting broccoli.
- Also winter chicory

HARVEST

- Courgettes, summer squashes, the first outdoor tomatoes, onions and globe artichokes, peppers cucumbers and aubergines
- Melons, plums, nectarines, last of the summer raspberries, blueberries and figs, early eating apples and plums

GENERAL TASKS

- **Prune out** any leaves that are shading tomato fruits
- **Cut and dry** or freeze herbs
- **Cut** fruited raspberry canes down to ground level. Any new canes will bear next year's crop
- **Keep an eye out** for brown rot in fruit trees. Cut off infected fruit and destroy

August project

Collect and save seeds

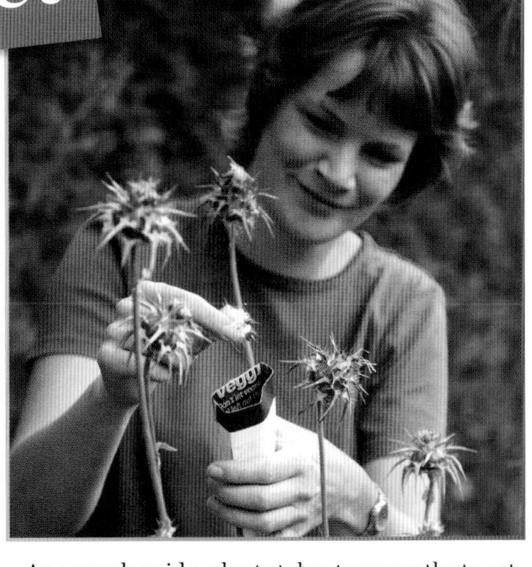

THE USUAL advice is to regularly deadhead flowering plants to encourage more blooms. This is because once a plant starts to set seed it concentrates all of its energy on producing offspring and flower production begins to shut down.

However, it's worth allowing a few plants to set seed – collecting seed from your favourite plants is one of the joys of gardening. It will also save you money as commercial seed is expensive.

Let a few of your plants go to seed from midsummer, then later on, let some of your late-season annuals produce seeds too.

TOP TIP
Save up little silica sachets that you get when you buy handbags and shoes and add them to your seed storage boxes to keep moisture away

As a rough guide, plants takes two months to set seed from flowering. The best time to collect seed is in the middle of the day, as pods are likely to be much drier then. Only select pods that look dry and show signs that they are about to crack open – immature seeds will not germinate. Annual seeds are normally kept and sown in March or April, but perennial seed, which takes longer to germinate, can be sown straightaway in trays or direct into the ground outdoors.

Before you venture out into the garden, make sure you've got everything you need – old paper bags or envelopes, a pencil, plant labels and a pair of scissors (or secateurs).

Step by step: How to collect seed

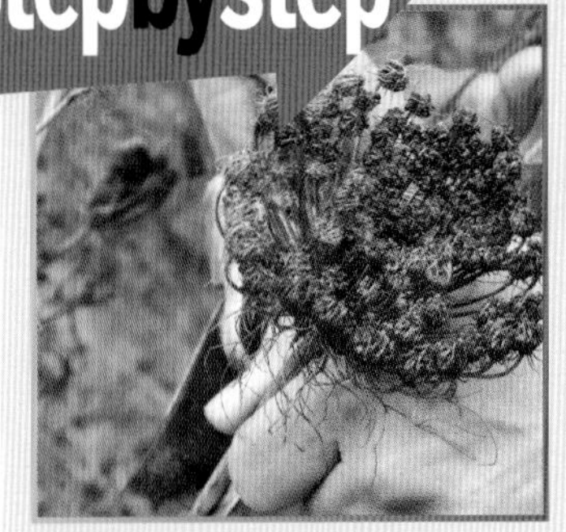

1 Shake seeds straight into a paper bag, or cut off seedheads and put them into the bags so they can finish off drying.

2 Tip the seeds out onto a sheet of paper and remove bits of debris or insects. Best done somewhere out of the wind.

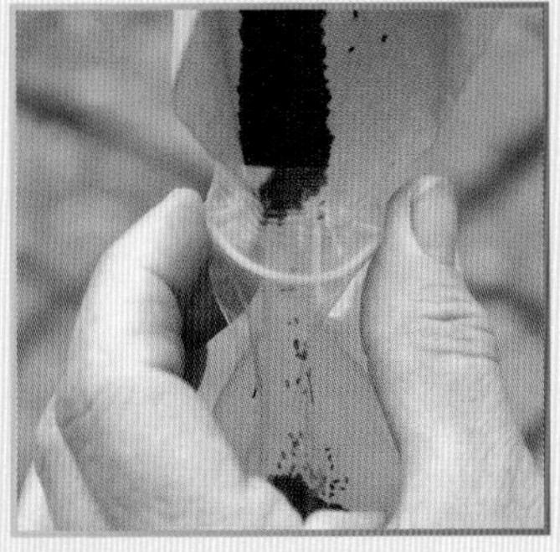

3 Funnel the seeds into labelled envelopes or bags Store somewhere cool and dry – the bottom of a fridge is ideal.

5 EASY FLOWER SEEDS TO SAVE

- ***Calendula***
- Digitalis purpurea
- ***Cosmos bipinnatus***
- Nicotiana sylvestris
- ***Lunaria annua*** (pictured below)

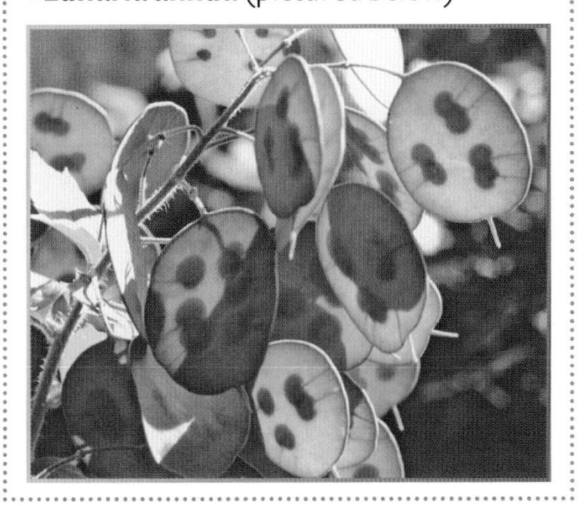

VARIABLE RESULTS

Sowing saved seeds is a bit of a lottery – you never quite know what you're going to get – but this is half the fun of it! A few species, like *Alchemilla mollis*, will produce plants that are exact replicas of themselves, but others, such as foxgloves and aquilegia, will readily cross with others, so results will be variable.

You'll definitely get variable results with hybrid seed (which has been bred by nurserymen for uniformity) but it's still worth having a go.

VEG & HERBS

Only save open-pollinated varieties and not hybrids. The Real Seed company **(www.realseeds.co.uk)** is an excellent source of these kinds of seeds **The following seeds are a good place to start:**

- **Heirloom tomatoes**
- **Pumpkins**
- **Coriander**
- **Parsley**
- **Peas (pictured below)**

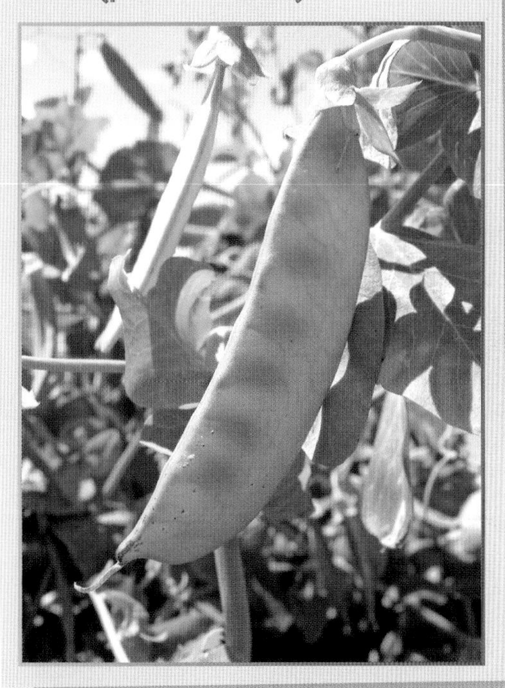

SEED SWAPPING

Once you start getting into seed saving you'll find it addictive and before you know it you'll have carrier bags full of seeds! But most gardeners don't have the space to sow 50 foxgloves for example, so only save the seeds you need. Consider starting a seed exchange with your neighbours.

SEPTEMBER

Summer is waning and autumn is approaching, but bedding plants should still be looking good if you've been keeping up with feeding and deadheading. If not, fill gaps with any spare bedding you've held in reserve for emergencies.

Once peas and beans have finished, remove top growth but leave the roots in place – the stored nitrogen will be released into the soil for next year. Continue to harvest other fruit and veg crops regularly – ease off the feeding of tomatoes and cucumbers as fruit production wanes.

Garden centres should be well stocked with spring bulbs like daffodils, crocus and hyacinths – they can be planted later this month and into October.

SEPTEMBER PLANTS

5 OF THE BEST

1 DAHLIA 'RIP CITY'

A semi-cactus type with gorgeous red-black blooms. Produces strong, healthy plants. Plant in bold groups for the best effect. Looks striking in the vase, too. **H4½ft (1.5m)**

2 SEDUM SPECTABILE 'BRILLIANT'

Succulent grey-green leaves topped with large flat pinkish purple flowerheads. Loved by bees and butterflies. Best at front of border. **H17in (43cm)**

3 PENNISETUM ALOPECUROIDES 'HAMELN'

Clump-forming compact grass, suitable for small gardens. Pretty brush-like flowerheads in autumn. Needs sun and well-drained soil. **H47in (1.2m)**

4 ASTER X FRIKARTII 'MÖNCH'

Masses of star-shaped, mauve flowers appear in July and carry on until October. Looks good alongside rudbeckia and pennisetum. **H 35in (90cm)**

5 RUDBECKIA FULGIDA VAR. SULLIVANTII 'GOLDSTURM'

Knee-high golden yellow daisy flowers from August to October. An easy-care plant that looks great in drifts alongside grasses. **H 35in (90cm)**

OTHERS TO TRY

- *Acer japonicum* 'Aconitifolium'
- *Anemanthele lessoniana*
- *Aster* 'Little Carlow'
- *Buddleja* x *weyeriana* 'Sungold'
- *Dahlia* 'David Howard'
- *Fuchsia triphylla* 'Thalia'
- *Gaura lindheimeri*
- *Hibiscus syriacus* 'Oiseau Bleu'
- *Miscanthus sinensis* 'Gracillimus'
- *Penstemon* 'Sour Grapes'
- *Phlox* 'Blue Evening'
- *Sanguisorba canadensis*
- *Salvia* 'Silas Dyson'
- *Solanum crispum* 'Glasnevin'
- *Rosa* 'Buff Beauty'
- *Verbena bonariensis*

SEPTEMBER 2014

MONDAY
1

TUESDAY
2

WEDNESDAY
3

THURSDAY
4

FRIDAY
5

SATURDAY
6

SUNDAY
7

MONDAY
8

AT A GLANCE
JOBS TO DO THIS MONTH

GENERAL TASKS

- ☐ Buy or make a compost bin for all the autumn debris (see p173).
- ☐ Cover ponds with netting to prevent falling leaves entering the water.

LAWNS

- ☐ Remove thatch (dead grass and moss) with a spring-tined rake.
- ☐ Aerate and top-dress.
- ☐ Feed lawns with autumn fertiliser to build them up for the winter.
- ☐ Sow new lawns from seed.

TREES, SHRUBS AND CLIMBERS

- ☐ Plant pot-grown trees and shrubs.
- ☐ Plant and move evergreens.
- ☐ Trim hedges like hornbeam, Leyland cypress, beech, thuja, *Lonicera nitida* and privet.

Start to clear garden debris

SEPTEMBER 2014

TUESDAY
9

WEDNESDAY
10

THURSDAY
11

FRIDAY
12

SATURDAY
13

SUNDAY
14

MONDAY
15

TUESDAY
16

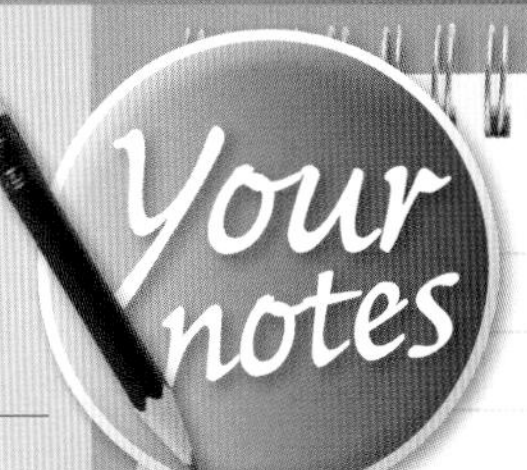

WEATHER:

PLANTS IN BLOOM:

TO DO:

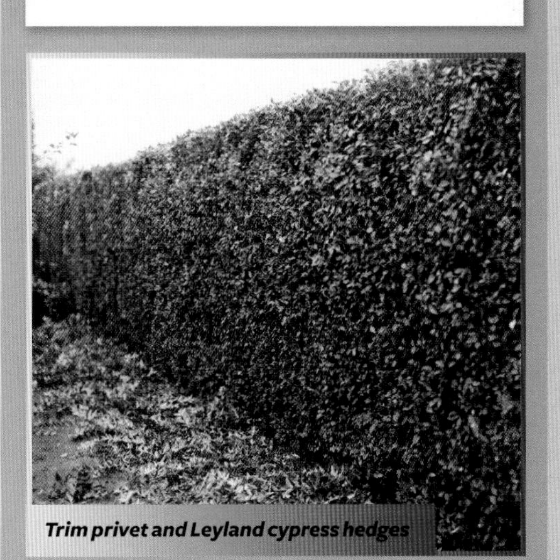

Trim privet and Leyland cypress hedges

SEPTEMBER 2014

WEDNESDAY
17

THURSDAY
18

FRIDAY
19

SATURDAY
20

SUNDAY
21

MONDAY
22

TUESDAY
23

WEDNESDAY
24

AT A GLANCE
JOBS TO DO THIS MONTH

FLOWERS

- [ ] Plant new perennials; cut down and divide existing ones.
- [ ] Plant daffodils and other spring bulbs.
- [ ] Sow hardy annuals outside for early flowering next year.
- [ ] Plant out spring-flowering biennials and winter-flowering pansies.
- [ ] Clear out summer bedding as it comes to an end.
- [ ] Continue to collect seed from perennials and alpines.

IN THE GREENHOUSE

- [ ] Move pots of tender plants like fuchsias and pelargoniums undercover.
- [ ] Sow hardy annuals in pots.
- [ ] Plant early spring bulbs in pots.
- [ ] Reduce watering and feeding of all greenhouse and container plants.

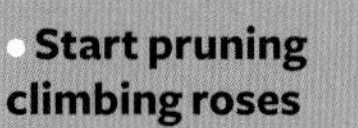

WHAT TO PRUNE

- **Start pruning climbing roses**
- **Prune lavender to maintain its shape**
- **Remove suckers from shrubs and the base of trees (pictured)**
- **Prune tall roses to reduce windrock**

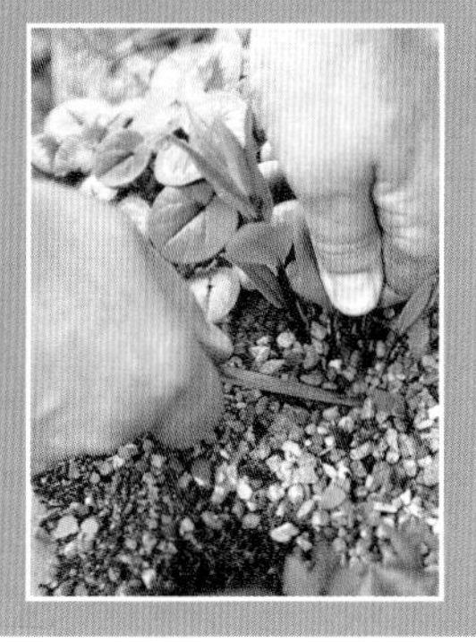

SEPTEMBER 2014

THURSDAY
25

FRIDAY
26

SATURDAY
27

SUNDAY
28

MONDAY
29

TUESDAY
30

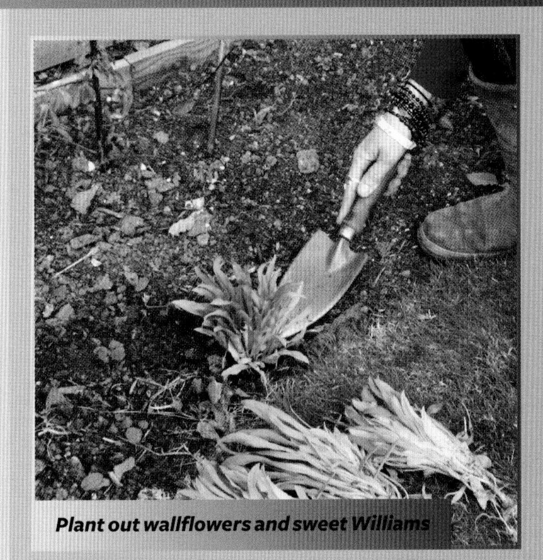
Plant out wallflowers and sweet Williams

WEATHER:

PLANTS IN BLOOM:

TO DO:

Plant out perennials

September is the ideal time to plant herbaceous perennials. Warm soil from summer together with frequent autumn rainfall helps plants to establish before winter sets in, ready to make new growth in spring. That said, if you garden on very wet, heavy soil or live in an area particularly prone to winter flooding, you are better off waiting until spring.

It's still important to follow the advice on the plant labels to help you choose the right plant for the right place. This includes checking whether they suit your soil type, and if they prefer sun or shade.

You also need to know the growth habit, height, spread and colour in order to visualise how the plants are going to fit into your border schemes. Lupins, delphiniums and hardy geraniums can all go in now. Occasionally perennials can be bought as bare-root plants but more commonly they're sold in 2-litre pots. Both types ideally should be planted out as soon as possible.

TOP TIP
If you find perennial plug plants for sale now, it's best to pot them on and wait until spring before planting out

Step by step: How to plant perennials

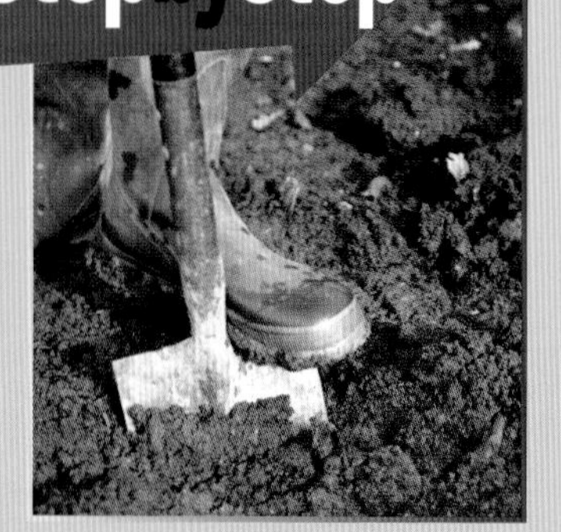

1 Prepare the border by forking it over; at the same time remove any weeds. Condition the soil by mixing in well-rotted garden compost or manure.

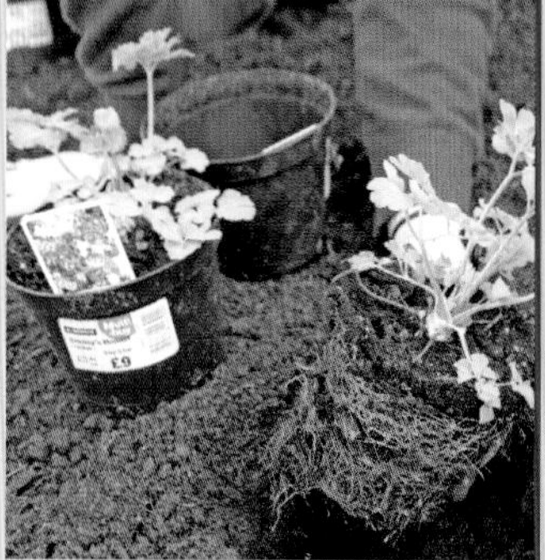

2 Dig a hole twice the width of the root ball and slightly deeper than the pot. Remove plant from its pot, tease out some roots. and place it in the hole.

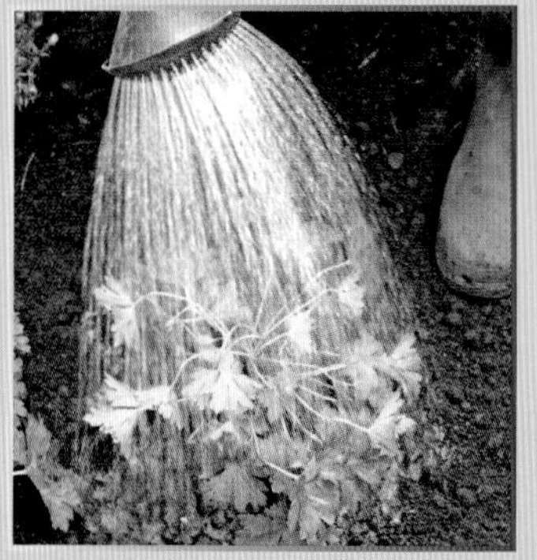

3 Check that it's at the same depth as it was in the pot. Refill soil around the edges, getting rid of any air pockets. Firm in well, then water thoroughly.

ON A BUDGET?

If you need to buy a lot of plants the cost will soon add up: expect to pay up to £10 for plants in two and three litre pots. Here are two money-saving ideas:

Buy wise: Often in late summer/early autumn there's a good range of cheaper plants in smaller 4in (10cm) pots. Don't forget to look out for multi-buy deals to keep costs down.
The great divide: This is the perfect time to lift and divide border plants – to get more plants for free! Even if you don't require new plants, most perennials should be divided every three years to keep them contained and healthy.

8 NECTAR-RICH PERENNIALS

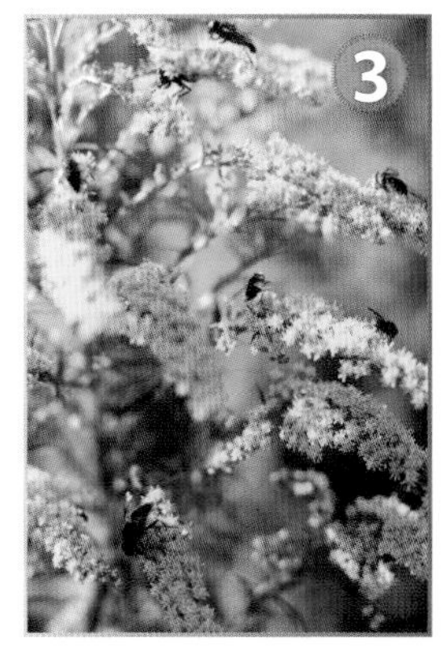

These late-season plants will not only allow you to enjoy a last flush of flowers, but local bees and butterflies will benefit too!

1 **ANCHUSA (*Anchusa officinalis*) –** delightful blue-purple flowers that curl like a scorpion's tail.

2 **BEE BALM (*Monarda* 'Squaw') –** most monardas are susceptible to mildew, so plant in the middle of a border to disguise lower leaves.

3 **GOLDENROD (Solidago)–** has dramatic arching sprays of tiny mimosa-like flowers.

4 **HELENIUM –** yellow to coppery red daisy flowers from summer to autumn.

5 **VALERIAN (*Centranthus ruber*) –** a cottage garden favourite brimming with nectar. Likes poor soil.

6 **OX-EYE CHAMOMILE (*Anthemis tinctoria*)** – produces masses of daisy flowers in shades of yellow.

7 **GLOBE THISTLE (*Echinops ritro*) –** this undemanding perennial has prickly bright blue flowerheads that are a magnet to bees and butterflies.

8 **MICHAELMAS DAISY (*Aster novi-belgii*) –** daisy flowers in reds, pinks, purples and blues.

How to store & preserve crops

After all the hard work you've put into growing fruit and veg over the summer months, you're likely to have a surplus of produce. Realistically you won't be able to consume all the crops you've harvested before they spoil – so storing and preserving is the answer.

The easiest crops to preserve are leeks and parsnips. These robust vegetables can be left in the ground over winter and harvested when needed. Protect the ground with straw or fleece to make them easier to dig up in frozen conditions. Potatoes and onions should be lifted and kept somewhere dry.

Soft crops that contain a lot of water need to be dealt with differently – tomatoes and berries for instance, can be frozen or turned into sauces and jams.

Pick crops when they're young for a better taste and to avoid gluts of large, mature veg

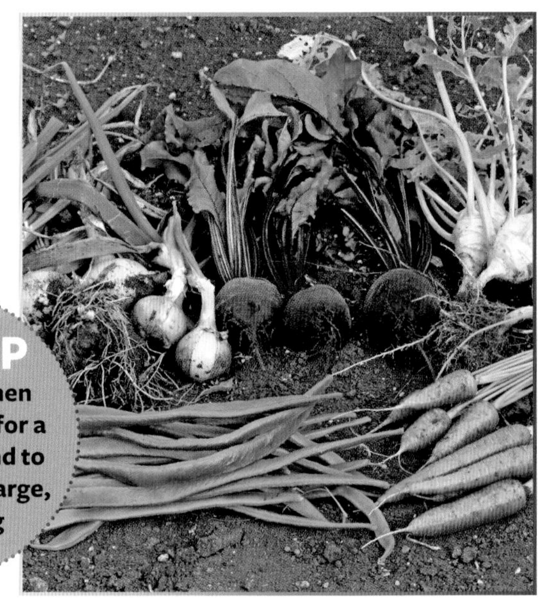

POTATOES

Don't delay lifting your spuds once the haulms (the above-ground stems and leaves) have died down. Lift the tubers on a dry day, and leave them on the surface of the ground for a short while to get rid of surplus moisture from the skins. Then place the dry potatoes into paper sacks or cardboard boxes taking care not damage or bruise them. The container should be breathable and exclude light. Storage is then somewhere dark, cool but frost-free, and protected from rodents.

ONIONS

Only lift onions once the foliage has died down completely. If any of the bulbs have thick necks, use them straight away as they won't store well. Don't bruise the bulbs during lifting. Let them dry off in full sun and protect from rain. Store onions for use during autumn and winter in trays, in dry, cool (but frost-free) conditions.

MAKE TOMATO SAUCE

1 To make one jar of sauce take eight ripe 'Roma' tomatoes, chop them up and add to a saucepan with a chopped onion. Cook over a low heat until soft.

2 Pass through a sieve or mouli into a large saucepan. Season with salt and pepper and dried Italian herbs, and add a teaspoon of sugar, and chopped garlic and fresh basil.

3 Cook for a further 20 minutes, then funnel the sauce into warmed, sterilised bottles or jars. Pour in half an inch of olive oil, which acts as a cap to prevent spoiling.

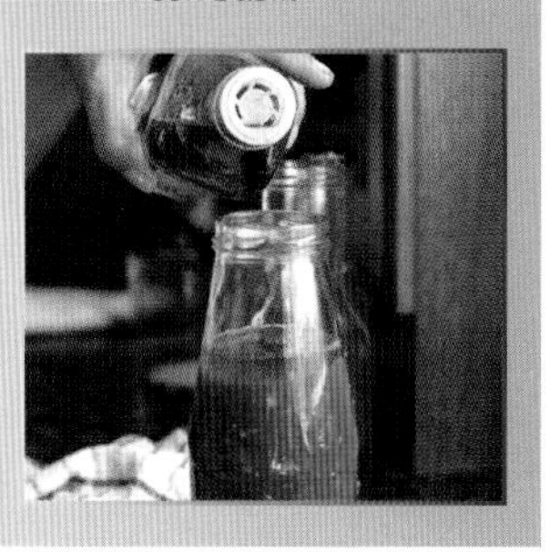

OTHERS TO TRY

- **Root crops** like carrots, swede and beetroot can be lifted and stored in crates of moist sand in a cool, frost-free place.
- **Runner beans** freeze well – chop into pieces and blanch in boiling water for two minutes beforehand.
- **Courgettes** are best used fresh, but you can turn gluts into chutneys & pickles.
- **Spread raspberries** out individually on a tray before freezing them to stop them mushing together, then put them into bags or boxes and return to the freezer.
- **Place unblemished apples** on newspaper in shallow cardboard boxes; make sure they aren't touching.

September

THE EDIBLE GARDEN - OTHER JOBS TO DO THIS MONTH

SOW

- Winter lettuce
- Green manures

PLANT

- Spring cabbages
- New strawberry plants
- Autumn onions sets

HARVEST

- Lift maincrop potatoes
- Pick pumpkins and squashes, sweetcorn and runner beans
- Pick first of autumn raspberries, apples and pears
- Last of the globe artichokes

GENERAL TASKS

- **Cut down** asparagus foliage once it turns yellow
- **Give leeks** a boost with a liquid feed of general fertiliser
- **Use up** what's in the compost bin so that there's room to add more waste as plants die back
- **Lift and divide** perennial herbs such as sage, chives and mint
- **Cure** pumpkins and squashes in the sun for several days to ripen before they go into storage; they should keep until well after Christmas

September project

Force hyacinth bulbs

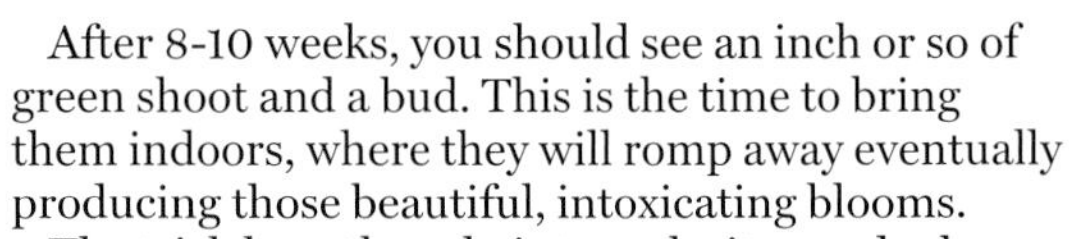

NOW IS the time to plant hyacinth bulbs so they'll bloom in time for Christmas. Hyacinth's normal flowering time is in the spring, but if you buy specially treated bulbs (look out for the word 'prepared' on labels), they'll think that winter has already passed and will begin to grow as soon as planted.

When it comes to choosing your bulbs, don't get hung up on varieties. There's little variation in flower shade and shape, and it often just comes down to a choice of pink, white or blue.

Plant them in compost 4in (10cm) deep, with their tops just poking out of the soil, and give them 8-10 weeks in the dark and cool (10°C/50°F) to persuade them to root. Not enough cold and you'll get a shoot but no root. This can be tricky to achieve with our much milder autumns. Try to find the coolest spot in the garden, such as burying them in a bed of sand under a north-facing wall, or putting them under a cardboard box in the garage. Hyacinths are vulnerable to frost though, so protect the pot if storing outside above ground.

After 8-10 weeks, you should see an inch or so of green shoot and a bud. This is the time to bring them indoors, where they will romp away eventually producing those beautiful, intoxicating blooms.

The trick here though, is to make it a gradual process (to mimic the onset of spring) – they won't like being brought into a centrally-heated home straightaway. Try them first in the coolest room of the house, and then once you start to see the flowerheads emerging, move them to their final pride of place.

If your hyacinths aren't quite ready in time for Christmas, don't worry – there are usually plenty of flowering ones in the shops to choose from in December.

Why not try timing your hyacinths to flower for January/February instead? With the post-Christmas lull and short, wintry days, what better way to pick your spirits up than with beacons of spring beaming out from the mantelpiece.

TOP TIP

Plant up hyacinth bulbs in individual 9cm pots, so that you can transfer them to your prettiest pots indoors once they've had their period of cold and green shoots are beginning to grow.

POTENTIAL PROBLEMS

- **Don't let the compost get too soggy or dry out**
- Don't remove the bulbs too soon from their cold, dark conditions
- **Make sure the dark conditions are cold enough (10°C/50°F)**

Step by step How to plant

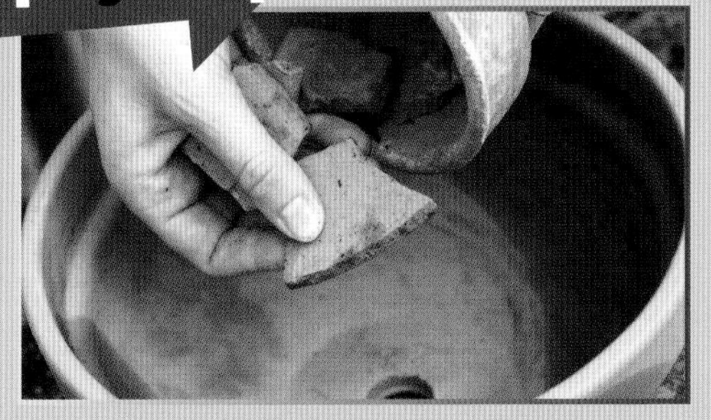

1 You can plant up prepared hyacinths in a pot with or without a drainage hole. If yours does have a hole, place crocks at the bottom of it.

2 Bulb fibre compost is the best medium to grow bulbs in. Only use multipurpose compost if your pot has a drainage hole.

3 Nestle the bulbs in the soil with enough space between them so that they aren't touching, and with the pointy tip facing upwards.

4 Aim to water the soil and not the bulbs. If the pot is soaked, leave it out in the sun to dry the bulb tops off before plunging them into darkness.

GROWING IN VASES

An alternative way to grow hyacinths is in special hyacinth vases. Fill with water up to the neck so that the bottom of the bulb is barely touching the water. Keep in the cool and dark for 8-10 weeks until you see a flower bud forming, then bring indoors.

OTHER BULBS TO FORCE

■ **'Paper White'** narcissi are another favourite to force now, and they'll flower in six weeks. Plant up the same way as hyacinths, with tips just above the soil's surface and keep in a cool, place – but not in the dark. The warmer they are, the quicker they'll shoot up, so try to keep them cool.

OCTOBER

The first frosts of autumn may not have struck yet, but shortening days and cooler conditions mean that flowers are on their way out. It's time to heave out the summer bedding and replace it with plants that will provide colour through winter: pansies, polyanthus and wallflowers.

If you planned things well, asters and chrysanthemums should be blooming now – make sure plenty of air can circulate between plants to keep mildew at bay.

You may still be harvesting fruit and vegetables; make sure everything's disease-free if you're going to store any.

OCTOBER PLANTS 5 OF THE BEST

1 CERATOSTIGMA PLUMBAGINOIDES

Hardy woody perennial with spectacular autumn colour and vivid blue flowers. **H15in (40cm)**

2 FUCHSIA 'MRS POPPLE'

Hardy fuchsia with lots of vibrant flowers from June to October. Grow in a sheltered spot. Top growth may be caught by frost but should revive itself by spring. **H43in (1.1m)**

3 ANEMONE 'HONORINE JOBERT'

Crisp white saucer flowers with bright yellow centres are a welcome sight in early autumn. Dislikes wet soil. **H4ft (H1.2m)**

4 ACER PALMATUM 'OSAKAZUKI'

One of the best Japanese maples for autumn colour. Can be grown in a border or a large pot.
H6ft (2m) after 10 years

5 COLCHICUM AUTUMNALE

Crocus-like pale-lilac blooms. Leaves don't appear until the spring, hence the common name, naked ladies. May be naturalised in turf. **H7in (20cm)**

OTHERS TO TRY

- *Abelia chinensis*
- *Acer palmatum* 'Sango-Kaku'
- *Amaryllis belladonna*
- *Colchicum* 'Waterlily'
- *Crataegus persimilis* 'Prunifolia'
- *Cyclamen hederifolium*
- *Euonymus* 'Red Cascade'
- *Liriope muscari*
- *Malus* 'John Downie'
- *Nandina domestica*
- *Physalis alkekengi* var. *franchetii*
- *Pyracantha* 'Soleil d'Or'
- *Rhus typhina*
- *Schizostylis coccinea* 'Major'
- *Tricyrtis formosana*
- *Viburnum opulus*

OCTOBER 2014

WEDNESDAY
1

THURSDAY
2

FRIDAY
3

SATURDAY
4

SUNDAY
5

MONDAY
6

TUESDAY
7

WEDNESDAY
8

AT A GLANCE
JOBS TO DO THIS MONTH

GENERAL TASKS

- ☐ Tidy borders and use the debris to make garden compost.
- ☐ Remove fallen leaves from lawns, the crowns of plants and pathways. Use them to make leaf mould (see p172).
- ☐ Reduce fish feeding and cut back pond plants that have gone over.
- ☐ Clean out the sludge at the bottom of ponds (once every five or six years).

LAWNS

- ☐ Reduce mowing frequency and raise the blades.
- ☐ Carry out autumn lawn care if you didn't get around to it last month.

TREES, SHRUBS AND CLIMBERS

- ☐ Prepare ground for planting bare-root trees and shrubs next month.

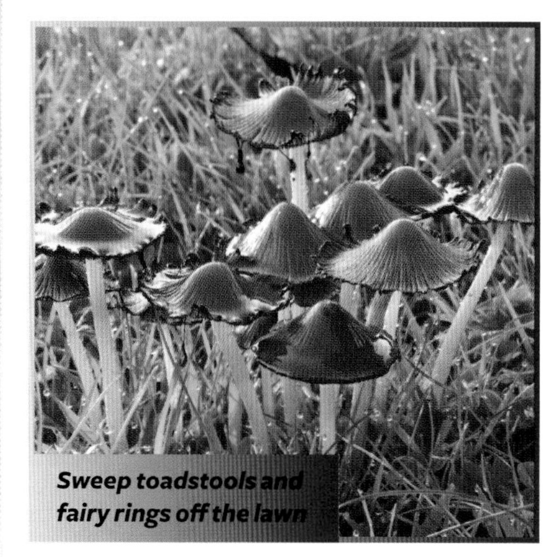

Sweep toadstools and fairy rings off the lawn

OCTOBER 2014

THURSDAY
9

FRIDAY
10

SATURDAY
11

SUNDAY
12

MONDAY
13

TUESDAY
14

WEDNESDAY
15

THURSDAY
16

Weed and spruce up paths and driveways

Your notes

WEATHER:

PLANTS IN BLOOM:

TO DO:

OCTOBER 2014

FRIDAY
17

SATURDAY
18

SUNDAY
19

MONDAY
20

TUESDAY
21

WEDNESDAY
22

THURSDAY
23

FRIDAY
24

AT A GLANCE
JOBS TO DO THIS MONTH

FLOWERS

- ☐ Dry attractive seedheads.
- ☐ Cut back herbaceous perennials that have finished flowering; plant new ones.
- ☐ Divide perennials (leave later-flowering ones like asters until the spring).
- ☐ If in a cold region, lift and store gladioli, dahlias, eucomis and tigridia.
- ☐ Move tender plants undercover.
- ☐ Plant new peonies and divide old ones.

IN THE GREENHOUSE

- ☐ Pot up cuttings taken in the summer.
- ☐ Pot up herbs like parsley and mint for winter use.
- ☐ If forced bulbs have top growth and root growth, bring them into the light.

CONTAINERS & PATIOS

- ☐ Plant up a winter container of pansies and polyanthus for colour on the patio.

WHAT TO PRUNE

- **Cut buddleja and lavatera back by half (hard prune in the spring)**
- **Continue pruning climbing roses**
- **Last chance to trim conifers (in the south)**

OCTOBER 2014

SATURDAY
25

SUNDAY
26

MONDAY
27

TUESDAY
28

WEDNESDAY
29

THURSDAY
30

FRIDAY
31

WEATHER:

PLANTS IN BLOOM

TO DO:

Brighten up pots and borders with winter pansies

'Winterize' the garden

The growing season for the vast majority of our garden plants is coming to a close. Now comes four months of 'down time' – deciduous trees and shrubs fall into dormancy, herbaceous perennials wither back to soil level, and spent summer bedding is hoiked out and relegated to the compost heap.

Evergreens really come into their own over the winter months, keeping the garden looking green and alive, and of course, there's all those lovely winter charmers like snowdrops, winter aconites and witchhazels to look forward to.

But before the garden goes into its slumber, we need to 'winterize it' – give it a good tidy up, wind it down and protect it from the ravages of winter weather. Here are 10 jobs that can to be tackled now:

10-STEP PLAN

1 Protect tender plants

Unless you're in a sheltered city garden, plants like bananas, tree ferns and cordylines should be protected at the first warning of frost – usually between September and November. Saw off the top growth of bananas, create a pyramid of canes over the stems, pack with straw and wrap with fleece.

2 Last chance to trim conifers

If we've had a mild autumn or you live in the south, you can get away with giving conifer hedges a final trim of the year to make them tidy and neat before winter sets in. It's important to keep these fast-growing trees in check with regular pruning but keep the trimming light to prevent bare patches.

3 Pond care

Use an old flowerpot to scoop out as much of the sludge at the bottom as you can. If your pond is stocked with fish, place a ba on the water's surface; this will keep an airhole open if i freezes. Switch off pumps t stop cold water circulating.

4 Cut back perennials

Trim back the withered stems of herbaceous plants that have finished flowering. Some, like teasels (pictured, right) produce attractive seedheads; if left on these can look stunning in winter frosts and also provide seeds for birds.

5 Dig empty areas of soil

If you have empty patches of soil in the veg plot or flower borders, dig them over now to expose the soil to the first frosts, which will break down clods of earth, helping to improve the soil's structure. Turning the soil will also help reduce diseases, and expose weed seeds and pests to birds.

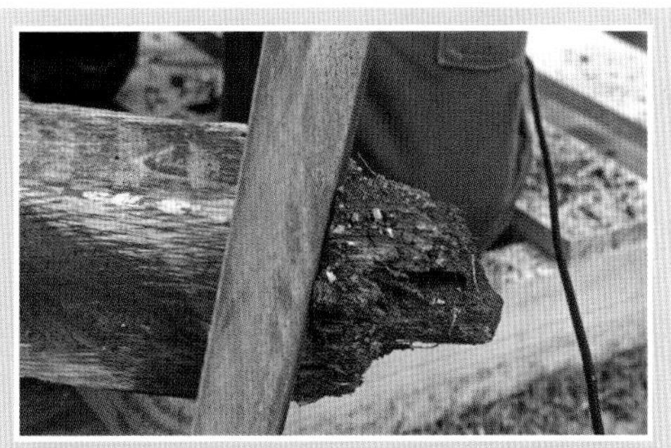

6 Check boundary fences

Make sure fence posts are not rotting off. A replacement now can save you having to replace the whole fence later on, plus whatever it smashes on the way down...

7 Heat the greenhouse

If heating the greenhouse over winter, set the thermostat on an electric heater to 37-39°F (3-4°C) so that it comes on automatically on cold nights to stop the temperature falling below zero. Pin bubble wrap over the glass inside to cut down on heat loss.

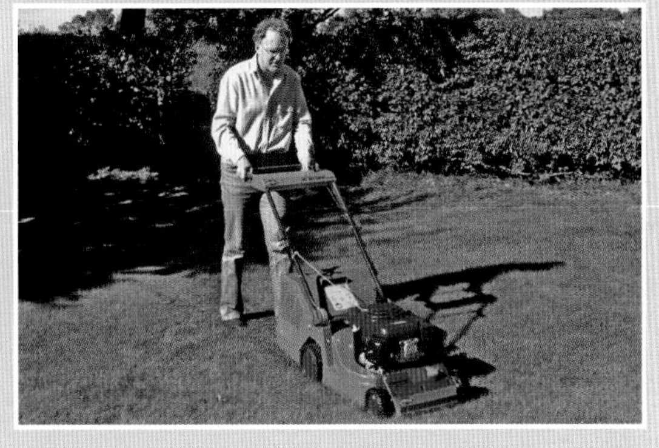

8 Lawnmower care

Before putting mowers into storage for the winter, run down the petrol and check blades for repairing. Clean and oil parts, too. If thinking of buying a new machine, look now as they are usually cheaper than in the spring.

9 Lift dahlias

When frost begins to blacken dahlia stems it's time to lift and store them. Cut them back to 6in (15cm), shake or rinse off soil and stand them upside down so that any moisture drains out of the hollow stems. Store them in boxes of dry compost.

10 Plant bulbs and bedding

There's still time to plant daffodil bulbs if you didn't last month. Crocus, alliums and fritillaries are best planted this month. Wait until next month to plant tulips. Plant pansies in border and containers for winter interest, and wallflowers for early spring colour next year.

Prune and tie-in climbing roses

Maintaining climbing roses is a lot more straightforward than you might think. Flowers are carried on the framework of mature wood, so you only need to prune the main stems if they have outgrown their allotted place. Otherwise, routine pruning simply entails shortening the sideshoots and taking out any dead, diseased and damaged wood. They're best pruned in the autumn, so that they can be tidied up and tied in before winter winds have a chance to thrash them about.

Tying in the stems is equally – if not more – important than pruning. In the wild, climbing roses flower at the very top of their stems – a special hormone within the plants prevents any flowers from forming further down the stems. In our gardens, we can manipulate climbing roses to flower further down by bending the stems into arch-shapes; this cuts off the hormone supply to the top, allowing flower production to happen all along the stems. If you don't have enough room to train shoots horizontally, go for a variety that is halfway between a tall shrub and a climbing rose, such as yellow-flowered 'Graham Thomas' (pictured), pink-flowered 'The Generous Gardener' or 'Crown Princess Margareta'.

TOP TIP

Don't prune climbing roses in their first two or three years, except to remove dead wood

Step by step: How to prune

1 Routine pruning involves cutting out dead, weak, diseased, and spindly wood. If the rose is heavily congested, cut out any really old branches from the base to promote new growth.

2 Then cut back sideshoots by two-thirds. Remove some new shoots to maintain the plant's symmetry. If main stems are too long, with few side-shoots, tip-prune them to the first strong bud.

3 Finally, tie in the new shoots, as well as loose or wayward shoots. Bend them horizontally rather than allowing them to go up into the air in order to encourage flowering the following year.

RENOVATING AN OLD CLIMBER

Occasionally, an old established climber will need to be given a new lease of life. Cut back one or two stems of older wood to 12in (30cm) from ground level. Repeat the process in subsequent years, so that you aren't hacking back all of the stems in one go. This can be carried out any time between late autumn and late winter.

RAMBLING ROSES

Ramblers are similar to climbers, but are more space-greedy and tend to flower only once, in June – but when they do they are smothered with blooms. Prune them in late summer, immediately after flowering. If you prune any later, you'll lose this year's flowers. Cut out about a third of the old stems at the base. Tie them in, too, as stems will become brittle later on in the year, making them less pliable. 'Phyllis Bide' (pictured) is a well-behaved repeat-flowering rambler.

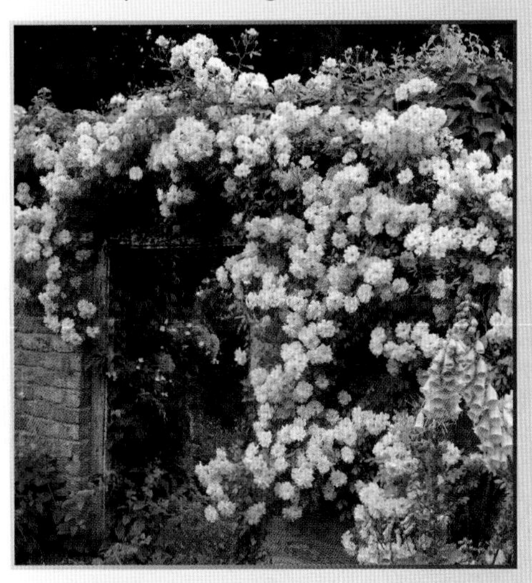

5 OF THE BEST CLIMBERS

1. **'Altissimo'** – unfading single flowers of bright red, with golden stamens.
2. **'Goldfinch'** – rambler with small buff-apricot flowers. Good fruity scent.
3. **'Crown Princess Margareta'** – is a tall, slightly arching shrub, can be trained as a short climber – good where space is restricted.
4. **'Mme Grégoire Staechelin'** – climber with clear pink, sweet pea-scented blooms.
5. **'Souvenier du Docteur Jamain'** – sumptuous claret-red roses. Good for a north-facing wall.

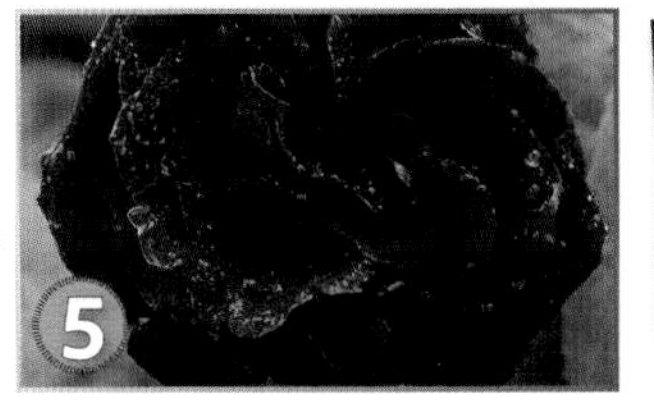

Don't forget!

It's also the start of the bare-root season. Roses (of all kinds, not just climbers) can be planted out now if you didn't get round to it earlier in the year.

Grow your own garlic

Garlic can be successfully grown across all regions of the UK provided it's given a rich, free-draining soil and is sited in an area that gets full sun.

You can plant garlic in autumn or early spring – but October is the ideal month, as garlic needs a long growing season and a period of cold (below 50°F/10°C) for good bulb development.

TOP TIP
Always buy certified 'seed' garlic bulbs. Do not use cloves from supermarkets as they may not grow as well

That said, if your soil is particularly heavy and wet, it's best to start garlic off in module trays filled with John Innes No1 compost. Insert the cloves individually into each cell, covering them with more compost. Keep them in a cool place, such as an unheated greenhouse or coldframe. Keep the compost moist but not wet. The young plants can be set out in spring when soil is workable.

HARDNECK OR SOFTNECK?

You'll often see bulbs sold as either hardneck or softneck. Hardneck garlic originates from colder climates and is the better choice for northern gardeners. It's considered by many to have a stronger, more interesting flavour – but on the downside, it won't store as long as softneck, and often needs to be consumed within a couple of months. Softneck garlic generally produces smaller, more tightly-packed cloves that are milder in flavour, and is the type you're most likely to find in supermarkets.

VARIETIES TO TRY

- **'Solent Wight':** Harvest late summer. Very good for storage
- **'Red Sicilian':** Hardneck with a spicy flavour, good for roasting. Harvest early summer
- **'Iberian Wight':** Large softneck. Good all-rounder. Plant a bit deeper than normal
- **'Lautrec Wight':** Hardneck suitable for autumn and early spring planting. Favoured by chefs

PLANT OUT

Make sure the cloves are the right way up – pointed end at the top. Use the biggest cloves, discarding any small ones, and plant 1-2in (3-4cm) below the surface with a spacing of about 7in (18cm) between them.

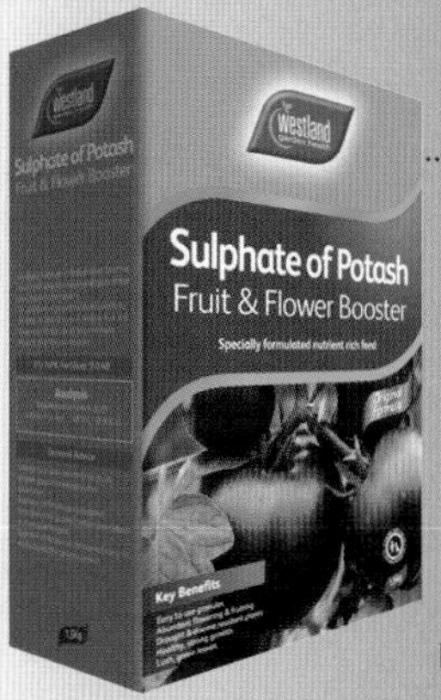

ROUTINE CARE

Once your crop is planted, it's straightforward to maintain. Keep the area weed free, and regularly water during the growing season. Apply sulphate of potash to autumn-grown crops in February to aid growth.

HARVEST

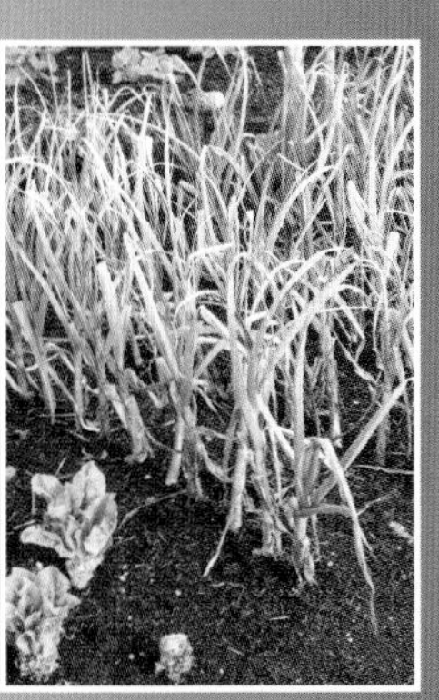

Autumn-planted garlic should mature by mid-summer. Stop watering during the last few weeks before harvest. Carefully dig out bulbs when foliage turns yellow (hardnecks) or begins to collapse (softnecks). Allow the bulbs to dry out in the sun or a shed before storing.

IN A CONTAINER

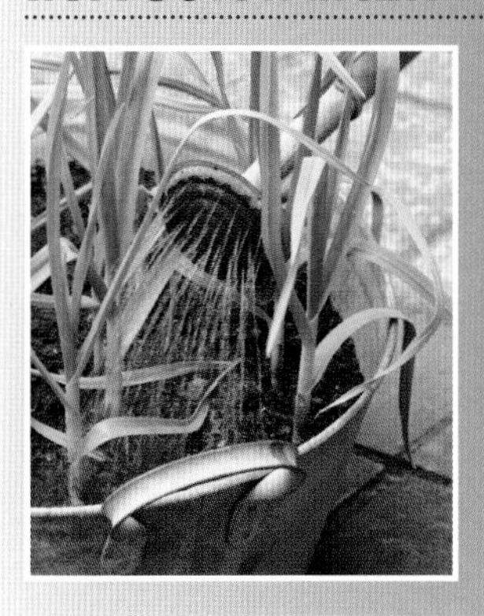

If you don't have a garden, garlic can be grown in a container. Use a free-draining soil based compost like John Innes No2 and keep the it well watered. As a rough guide, plant 6 cloves to a 11in (30cm) container.

October

THE EDIBLE GARDEN - OTHER JOBS TO DO THIS MONTH

SOW

- Sow broad beans outside (cover initially with a cloche to protect from mice and cold)

PLANT

- Spring cabbages and autumn onion sets

HARVEST

- Last of the runner beans
- Finish picking apples and lifting maincrop potatoes
- Ripen tomatoes indoors
- Pick homegrown grapes

GENERAL TASKS

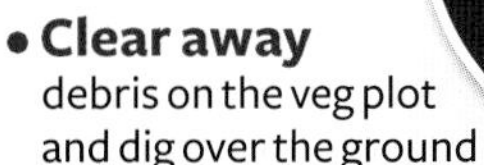

- **Clear away** debris on the veg plot and dig over the ground
- **Empty the compost bin** onto the soil and dig it in to replenish nutrients
- **Order new fruit trees** (bare-root) to ensure you get what you want
- **Protect salad crops** – winter lettuce, chard and spinach can be kept going through winter
- **Net brassicas** and remove yellow leaves
- **Re-pot fruit** trees and bushes in patio containers every year until they are full sized

October project

Cut flower chrysanths

Images and words: with many thanks to www.sarahraven.com

CHRYSANTHEMUMS ARE invaluable for flowering when everything else is going over (August to November) and they make fantastic cut flowers for the house, lasting up to three weeks.

Some varieties will only grow indoors where there's no risk of weather-damage, but most will happily grow outdoors, provided they're in full sun and shelter, and in well-drained soil with plenty of organic matter.

Only plant out young plants once all threat of frost has passed – towards the end of May – and after the plants have finished flowering, either dig them up and bring the whole root inside to propagate from in early spring, or mulch them deeply to get them through the winter (in mild regions).

If you have the facility to grow chrysanthemums in a greenhouse or protected growing space of some kind, you'll be able to enjoy gorgeous cut flowers from September right up until Christmas.

TOP TIP

For healthy plants and the best flowers, grow chrysanthemums from fresh cuttings taken every spring

HOW TO GROW UNDERCOVER

- **If you have soil beds in your greenhouse, rooted cuttings can be planted direct at spacings of 12-16in (30-40cm) and watered in well – or grow them in large containers, about 13-16in (35-40cm) in diameter.**
- Fill these containers with John Innes No 2 compost and plant one cutting per pot. Water in well. Insert a stake at their side, which you'll need to tie them to as they grow.
- **Place containers outside in a sunny, sheltered spot (after frost has finished).**
- Cut off the tops of plants down to 3 or 4 leaves from the base of the plant, 10-14 days after planting. This encourages side branches, which will form the flowering stems.
- **Water freely during the summer and give them a balanced feed every two weeks from midsummer until the flower buds start to appear.**
- Then bring inside again in September before the autumn gales arrive.
- **Pick the flowers from there.**

Step by step How to take cuttings

1 Remove a few of the stems, 2-3in long, from as near the base of the mother plant as you can.

2 Pinch out the growing tip, remove lower leaves and push them into a gritty mix of compost.

3 Place inside a clear plastic bag or in a heated propagator. Keep the compost moist at all times and they should root in three to four weeks.

WHICH ONES TO GROW?

The following chrysanthemums are available from **www.sarahraven.com**. Cuttings are despatched from April.

■ **Shaggy-headed:** Stylish, interesting shapes of chrysanthemums in the deepest, richest colours. Can be grown outdoors or indoors. If planted in May you'll have flowers from September.

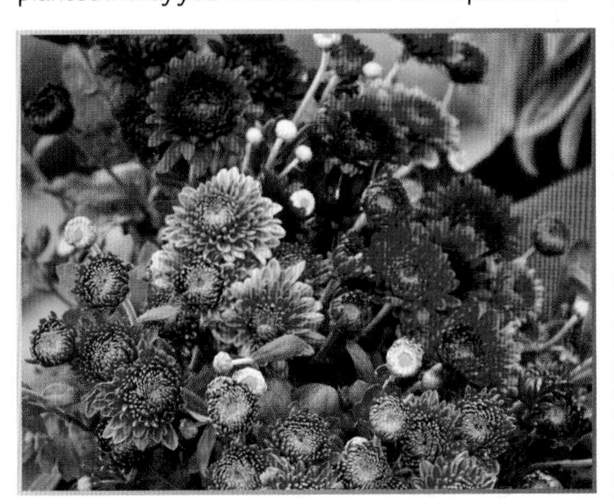

■ **Jewel chrysanthemums:** Gem-like colours, fantastic for filling jugs and vases with abundance for the last four months of the year. Can be grown inside or out.

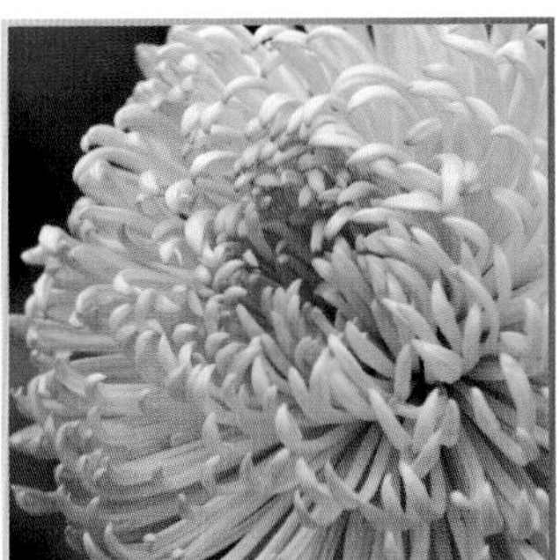

■ **'Anastastia Green'** Wonderful with all other chrysanthemum colours. Best grown indoors or moved into a greenhouse before the first frosts strike.

NOVEMBER

Mid-autumn can be kind, with mild, misty days and cool, calm nights, or it can be wild, with ferocious storms barrelling in from the Atlantic. If you didn't get around to it last month – check the state of your fencing before windy weather does any damage.

It's the start of the bare-root planting season, when deciduous trees and shrubs can be planted or moved in their dormant, leafless state so wrap up warm and get out on clement days. Press on with winter digging of the veg patch and plan what crops you'd like to grow next year.

In the flower borders, ornamental grasses backlit by low sunshine and lipstick-coloured berries keep the show going. If your garden is looking little drab, plant cheery containers of cyclamen, gaultheria and ornamental kale (pictured) for instant colour.

NOVEMBER PLANTS

5 OF THE BEST

1 NERINE BOWDENII

Lily-like bulb that provides a wonderful shock of bright pink flowers in autumn when everything else is dying back. Needs free-draining soil and shelter. **H2ft (60cm)**

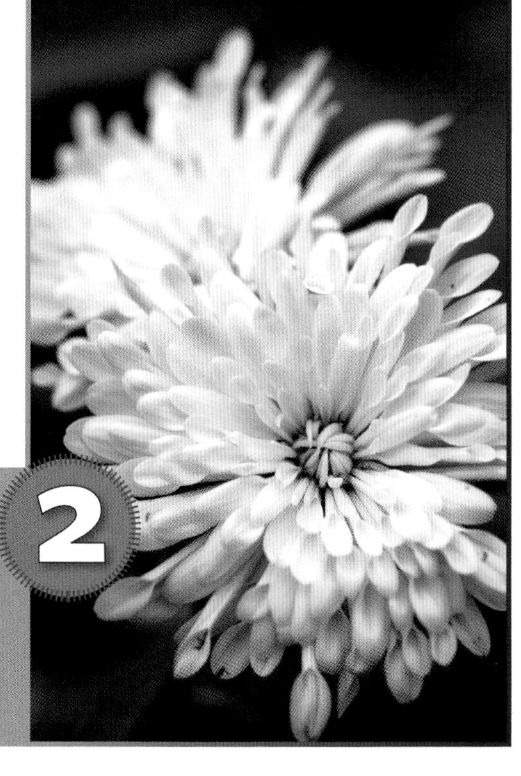

2 CHRYSANTHEMUM 'EMPEROR OF CHINA'

Particularly late flowering hardy chrysanth, in November and December. Red autumn leaves and soft-pink flowers. **H4ft (1.2m)**

3 MISCANTHUS SINENSIS 'KLEINE SILBERSPINNE'

Compact yet dramatic, this grass is perfect for smaller plots. Lovely when the evening sun catches the feathery silver plumes. **H4ft (1.2m)**

4 CALLICARPA BODINIERI 'PROFUSION'

A fairly nondescript plant throughout the year but its unusual autumn purple berries and red-tinted foliage make it worth the wait. **H9ft (3m)**

5 COTINUS COGGYGRIA 'GRACE'

Summer flowers that look like a haze of smoke are followed by stunning autumn foliage. For extra large leaves and to keep size in check, hard prune in early spring. **H19ft (6m).**

OTHERS TO TRY

- *Arbutus unedo*
- *Camellia sasanqua* 'Crimson King'
- *Clematis cirrhosa* 'Bill MacKenzie'
- *Cortaderia selloana* 'Pumila'
- *Iris foetidissima*
- *Prunus x subhirtella* 'Autumnalis'
- *Prunus serrula*
- *Rosa moyesii*
- *Viburnum davidii*
- *Vitis coignetiae*

NOVEMBER 2014

SATURDAY
1

SUNDAY
2

MONDAY
3

TUESDAY
4

WEDNESDAY
5

THURSDAY
6

FRIDAY
7

SATURDAY
8

AT A GLANCE
JOBS TO DO THIS MONTH

GENERAL TASKS

- [ ] Continue digging over veg patch and any other empty beds.
- [ ] Make leaf mould from fallen leaves.
- [ ] Order seed catalogues.
- [ ] Clean out bird boxes and feeders.
- [ ] Check for anything that's at risk from cold, wind or waterlogging.
- [ ] Last chance to protect tender plants.
- [ ] Lag outside taps to prevent freeezing.

LAWNS

- [ ] Only mow lawns if needed and keep the blades high.
- [ ] Last chance to lay new turf.

TREES, SHRUBS AND CLIMBERS

- [ ] Plant bare-rooted deciduous trees, shrubs and roses.
- [ ] Take hardwood cuttings of cornus, roses, weigela, buddleja and forsythia.

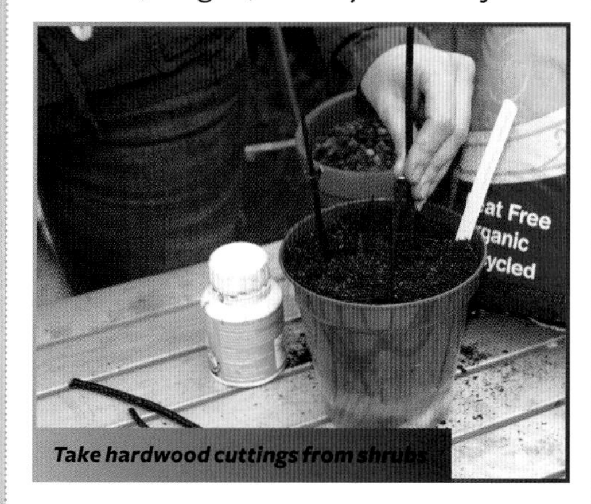

Take hardwood cuttings from shrubs

NOVEMBER 2014

SUNDAY
9

MONDAY
10

TUESDAY
11

WEDNESDAY
12

THURSDAY
13

FRIDAY
14

SATURDAY
15

SUNDAY
16

Clean out bird feeders and stock with fresh seed

Your notes

WEATHER:

PLANTS IN BLOOM:

TO DO:

NOVEMBER 2014

MONDAY
17

TUESDAY
18

WEDNESDAY
19

THURSDAY
20

FRIDAY
21

SATURDAY
22

SUNDAY
23

MONDAY
24

AT A GLANCE
JOBS TO DO THIS MONTH

FLOWERS

- [ ] Plant tulip bulbs (traditionally between Bonfire night and Christmas).
- [ ] Check stored bulbs, corms and tubers for rot.
- [ ] Start amaryllis into flower at beginning of month.
- [ ] Protect alpines from heavy rain with an open-ended cloche.

IN THE GREENHOUSE

- [ ] Continue to sow hardy annuals.
- [ ] Sow sweet peas for overwintering.
- [ ] Keep good air circulation around chrysanthemums to avoid mildew.

CONTAINERS & PATIOS

- [ ] Move pots into shelter by the house.
- [ ] Ensure pots are standing on pot feet to prevent waterlogging.

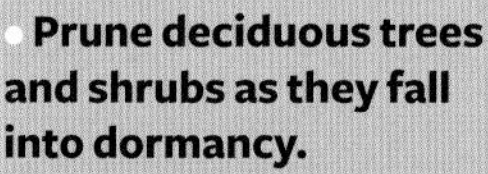

- **Prune deciduous trees and shrubs as they fall into dormancy.**
- **Prune back bush roses by a one third, to avoid wind rock (pictured)**
- **Trim summer-flowering heathers**

NOVEMBER 2014

TUESDAY
25

WEDNESDAY
26

THURSDAY
27

FRIDAY
28

SATURDAY
29

SUNDAY
30

WEATHER:

PLANTS IN BLOOM:

TO DO:

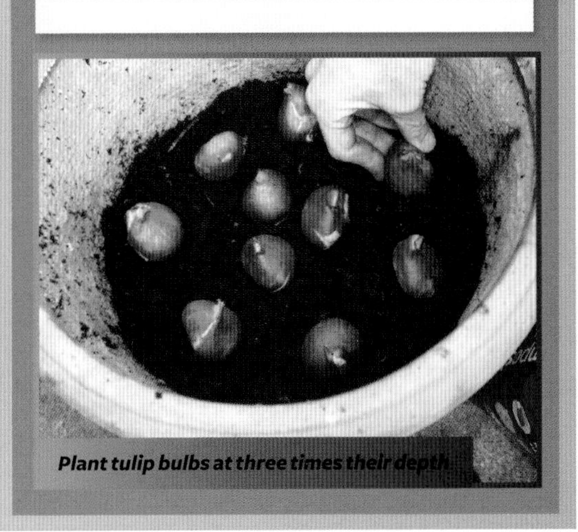
Plant tulip bulbs at three times their depth

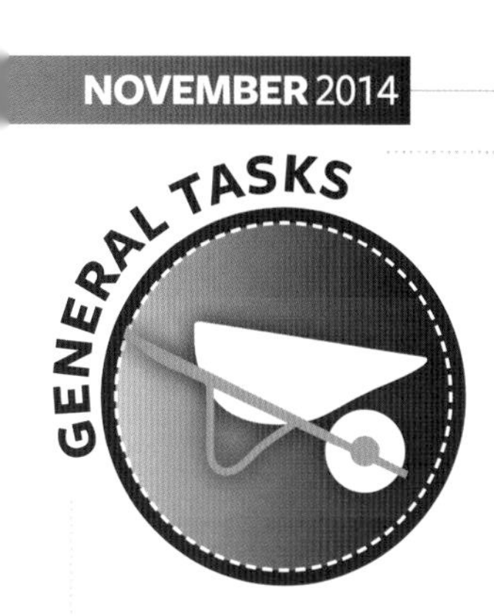

Make compost & leaf mould

All the gardening books and magazines emphasis the importance of adding 'organic matter' to the soil, but what is it and how do we obtain some? In a gardening context, organic matter is dead plant material and kitchen waste that has been rotted down to make compost or leafmould; it also includes well-rotted cow and horse manure and green manures.

Our garden plants regularly take up nutrients from the soil in order to grow strongly, therefore it makes sense to put back into the soil what is taken out of it. In wild habitats – like a forest – this occurs naturally, with dead matter and fallen leaves rotting back down into the ground. But in our gardens, this natural process is interrupted by us clearing away grass clippings, prunings and fallen leaves.

One of the best gardening practices you can get into is to regularly turn 'garden waste' into compost and leafmould. Even if you only make a couple of wheelbarrows-full of homemade compost each season, your plants will thank you for it.

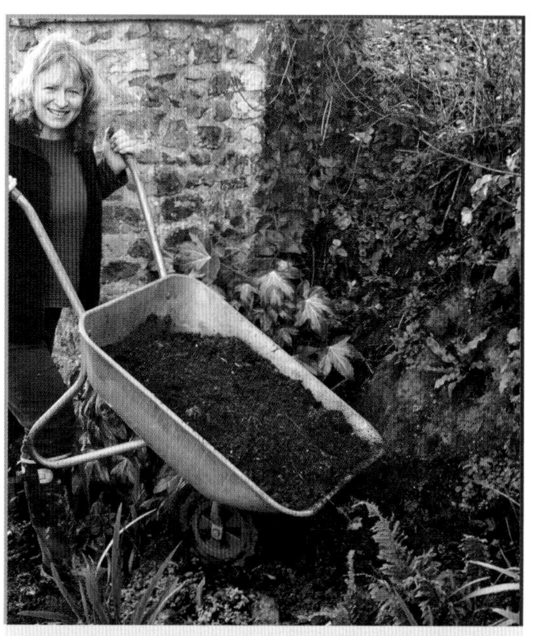

The ideal time to spread organic matter on the garden is early spring, when most plants are actively growing

LEAF MOULD

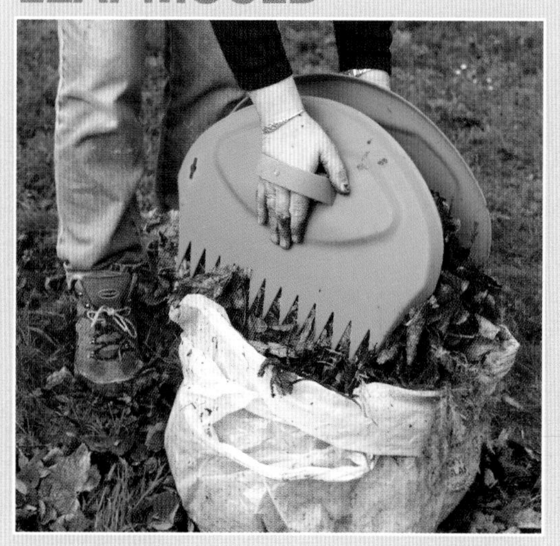

HOW TO MAKE IT

Fallen autumn leaves can be collected up and turned into a valuable soil conditioner – so keep them separate from the compost heap. Pack the leaves into bin liners to rot in a quiet corner for 18 months. Puncture the bags and shake them every now, as leaves need air in order to decompose.

- Alternatively, consider making a 'leaf bin'. Hammer four wooden stakes into the ground in a square shape. Wrap chicken wire around the frame and fix in place with wire. Keep the leaves moist to aid decomposition.

WHERE TO USE IT

Spread around plants in the border as a protective mulch, or dig it in to improve the soil's structure. Really well-rotted leaf mould can be used as part of a general potting compost or seed sowing mix.

Step by step Garden compost...in 3 easy steps

1 Buy or make a bin (there are benefits and drawbacks to all) and put it in an accessible location away from the house (they attract fruit flies) with room around the bin for mixing or chopping materials. Place it on the soil so compost creatures can pass freely between the heap and the earth.

2 Fill the bin with one part carbon-rich or 'brown' material, such as tough vegetable stems, shredded paper and woody prunings, to two parts nitrogen-rich or 'green' material such as vegetable peelings, cut flowers, grass clippings and young annual weeds (not gone to seed).

3 Turn the compost bin every so often. If it gets too slimy add more 'brown' material. If it gets too dry add 'green' material. Heaps will rot slowly during the cold part of the year and with no turning; with regular turning in the warmer months, you can achieve compost in as little as 12 weeks.

WHAT ABOUT SHOP-BOUGHT FERTILISERS?

It's possible to keep plants going just by feeding them with fertilisers, but for long-term plant health, you must also regularly add organic matter to the soil. Synthetic feeds like Growmore are convenient and quick-acting, but they won't condition and improve the soil's structure like bulky organic matter does, and are likely to be washed out of the soil faster.

LOCAL COUNCIL COMPOST

If you don't have the facilities or inclination to make your own compost, let your local council do it for you. Many offer green bin schemes, where they will take away your garden waste to be composted on large-scale specially-designated sites. If you're lucky, your council may even have a system where they sell back garden compost made from your green waste.

Plan your veg plot

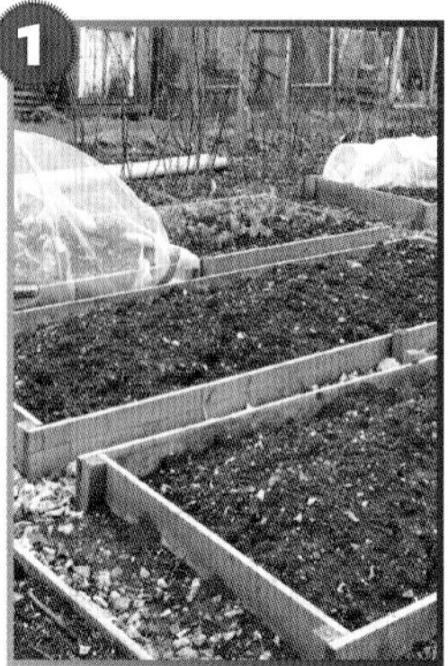

SETTING UP

Successful veg needs to be grown in soil that is well-structured and fertile. Veg growers dig over their soil between November and March, incorporating organic matter as they go, so that the winter weather can break down clods of earth into friable soil. Avoid trees as they block out sunlight while roots compete for nutrients and moisture in the soil. Steer clear of frost-pockets and windy sites, too.

The bigger your plot, the more veg you can grow, but those with smaller plots shouldn't feel hard done by: you can still grow the same range of crops, just in lower yields and you'll need to get creative with how you fit them into your space. Climbing or trailing crops like runner beans and squashes can be trained up wall trellis, and bush tomatoes, herbs, salads and mini veg varieties can all be grown in pots.

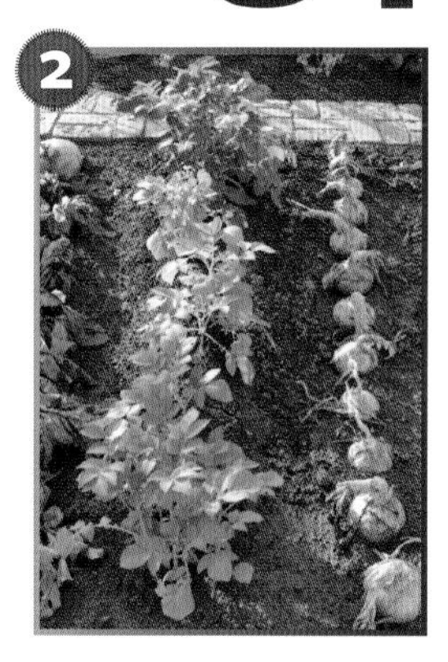

CROP ROTATION

To give your crops the best chance of remaining in good health, plan a crop rotation scheme. It's beneficial to put crops with similar nutritional requirements and pest problems together – but always grow these groups on different sites each year. This helps to avoid a build-up of pests and diseases in the soil that target a particular group of veg. Three popular groups are **brassicas** (cabbages/cauliflowers/calabrese/Brussels sprouts), **legumes** (peas/French beans/runner beans/broad beans) and **alliums** (leeks/onions/garlic/shallots).

Bigger plots can house larger rotations, but whatever the size of your plot, ensure that the same group isn't grown on the same site for three years. If space is too limited for crop rotation, grow veg in containers but always use fresh compost.

ORGANIC OR NOT?

Organic gardening (growing without peat, man-made fertilisers or chemicals) has become popular but takes more skill and patience than using conventional techniques.

Many people want to grow their own to ensure their crops are pesticide-free, although there has been some debate as to whether organic produce is tastier or more beneficial in terms of nutrients. The organic approach is all about striking a balance – growing plants strongly in good soil, encouraging natural predators into the garden, distracting pests with companion planting.

Chemical pesticides must always be used with care. Check that your chosen spray is approved for the type of fruit or vegetable that you intend to use it on. Aim to spray in the evening, when beneficial insects have stopped flying.

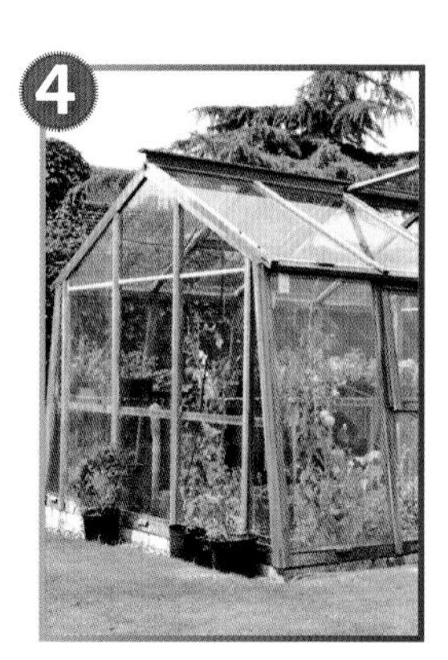

UNDERCOVER

A greenhouse lengthens the growing season, and allows you to grow warm-climate crops like tomatoes, aubergines, melons, chillies and peppers more reliably.

Small greenhouses are available for compact plots and mini-plastic ones can easily be packed away when not in use. It's even possible to grow chillies and tomatoes on a sunny windowsill.

When buying a greenhouse, make sure it comes with adequate roof vents. Movement of air and regulation of temperature is vital. Lack of good ventilation can lead to disease outbreaks and unhealthy crops. Always buy the largest structure you can. Ask any gardener what their biggest bugbear is, and they will often say running out of space!
Site in a sunny location (never near trees) and bolt to a sturdy base to avoid it shifting in gales.

Sow seeds | Plant or transplant | Harvest

	Jan	Feb	Mar	Apr	May	Jun	Jul	Aug	Sep	Oct	Nov	Dec
Asparagus				Harvest from year 3								
Beetroot			Indoors									
Broadbeans												
Brussels sprouts												
Calabrese												
Carrots												
Cauliflower		Indoors										
Chinese cabbage												
French beans			Indoors									
Jerusalem artichokes												
Leeks												
Lettuce												
Onions (winter)												
Parsnips												
Peas												
Potatoes												
Radishes		Indoors										
Rhubarb												
Runner beans												
Salad leaves			Indoors									
Spinach												
Spring onions												
Squashes				Indoors								
Sweetcorn												
Sweet peppers			Indoors									
Tomatoes		Indoors										

November project

DIY bird feeders

DESPITE THERE being plenty of berries on plants through autumn and winter, birds will appreciate some extra help in sourcing food supplies, at a time of year when they need it most.

Making these projects involves healthy winter walks in search of berries, threading bead-like berries into bracelets and kneading balls of gloopy fat. If you don't have easy access to the countryside, your garden may be a good source of sorbus, pyracantha or berberis. Other key ingredients you may already have in your kitchen cupboards – if not, they can easily be found in local shops.

Just follow the simple instructions and you'll have beautiful and unique outdoor ornaments to adorn your borders, boughs and branches. They make attractive and imaginative alternatives to plastic feeders and will cost less, too.

Choose from a variety of fillings and ingredients to provide different nutritional benefits to a wide range of garden birds. Sunflower seeds are rich in oil attracting sparrows, chaffinches, sparrows and tits. Suet and lard makes a high-energy food for wrens, blue tits and house sparrows and acts as a glue for other useful treats. Stir in tiny crab apples to attract robins, starlings and greenfinches. Rose hips are also enjoyed by many bird types – so if you grow *Rosa rugosa*, don't prune after its finished flowering and let it reward you with pretty hips.

If you don't have any suitable garden fruits or berries, shop-bought raisins are a fine alternative. Commercial seed mixes, developed by the experts are also worth turning to.

Hang feeders from tree branches

Styling: Helen Riches

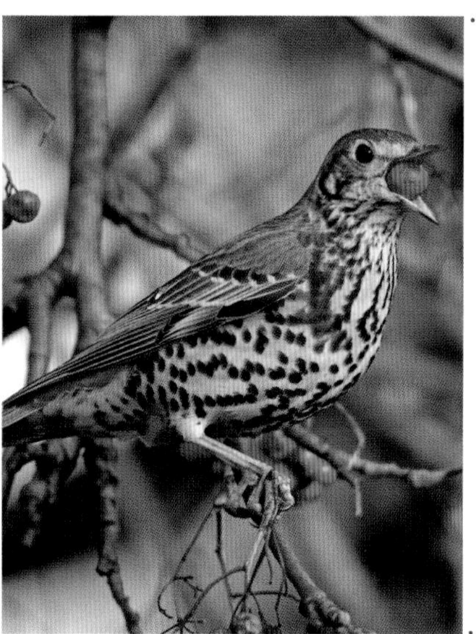

TOP BERRIES FOR BIRDS

- **Ivy**
- **Rose hips**
- **Cotoneaster**
- **Berberis**
- **Pyracantha**
- **Hawthorn**
- **Blackthorn**
- **Sorbus**
- **Bullace**
- **Malus**

Flowerpot cups look good in the borders

Berry Bracelets

You'll need:

- 0.7mm glavanised wire
- 2mm wire to punch holes in the tougher skinned types – or use a skewer
- Coloured jute twine – available from local craft shops
- A selection of berries such as: rosehips, sloe, rowan, cotoneaster and pyracantha

Bend the wire to make star-shapes, hearts or just simple circles. Don't be tempted to eat any of the berries yourself.

How to do it:

1 Thread on berries of your choice by piercing them. Caution: the insides of rosehips can be an irritant.

2 Twist ends of the wire together to close up bracelet. Tie on string, which can be as long as you choose.

Bird fat baubles

You'll need:

- Coloured jute twine from craft shops
- 1 cup of lard
- 1 cup of beef suet
- Large black sunflower seeds

Make these as novel, homemade Christmas gifts. Pop the mixture in the fridge if everything is getting sticky.

How to do it:

1 Melt lard and suet together. Allow to cool. Shape into balls. Slice half way and lay the string in the cut.

2 Reform the ball and set in the fridge. Stud with sunflower seeds. and hang from the branches of trees.

Flower Pot Cups

You'll need:

- x3 3ft (1m) hazel stakes – they must fit snugly into flowerpot holes
- 8oz (250g) lard and 7oz (200g) shredded suet
- Rosehips, crab apples, berries, raisins and bird seed
- Bowl for mixing

Plastic pots, bamboo canes and commercial seed mixes work just as well as terracotta pots, hazel stakes and berries.

How to do it:

1 Poke the thin end of the stake through the pot hole. Trim end of stick so it's level with top of pot.

2 Melt lard and suet. Leave to cool. Stir in chosen berries or seed. Pack mixture into pot.

DECEMBER

If your greenhouse is full of young plants that were taken as cuttings earlier in the year you'll want to keep it frost-free. Paraffin or gas is fine if you have no power supply, but an electric fan heater is more reliable and will cut in and out rather than staying on all night.

If top fruits pests were a problem this year apply a winter wash now – it'll get rid of them and their eggs. Apples and pears can be winter pruned on clement days. In the veg garden it's best to stay off the soil, especially if it's frozen or waterlogged, but it can still be worked if needed.

Towards the end of the month, place a couple of colourfully planted winter pots either side of the front door to greet your Christmas guests; battery-operated LED lights are a great way to add instant festive glamour.

DECEMBER PLANTS

5 OF THE BEST

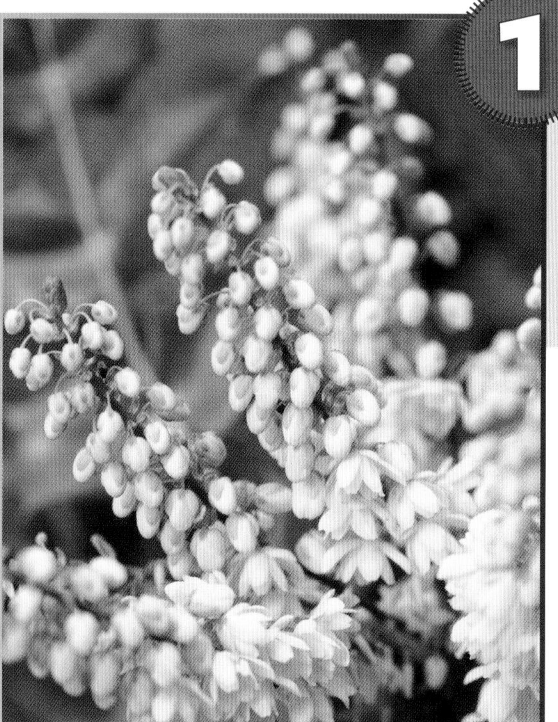

1 MAHONIA X MEDIA 'CHARITY'

Handsome holly-like evergreen leaves provide structure in the borders. Gorgeously scented yellow flowers from November to March. **H16ft (5m)**

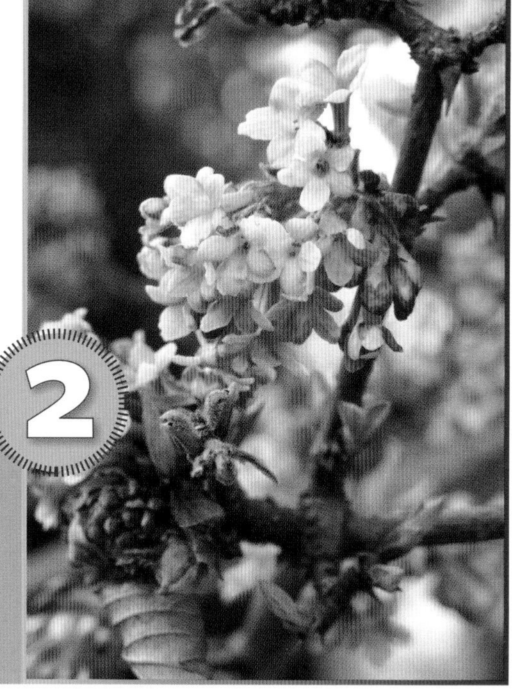

2 VIBURNUM X BODNANTENSE 'DAWN'

Deciduous shrub with a staggeringly long flowering period. Its clusters of sweet-scented blooms are held on naked stems from November to March. **H9ft (3m)**

3 HEDERA COLCHICA 'SULPHUR HEART'

Much more exciting than traditional English ivy, with large gold-splashed lime-green leaves. Good for livening up a shady wall or fence. **H16ft (5m)**

4 SARCOCOCCA HOOKERIANA VAR. DIGYNA

Compact evergreen with highly scented small tassel-like flowers. Good for growing in a pot, although will need planting out later on. **H4½ft (1.5m)**

5 ILEX X ALTACLERENSIS 'GOLDEN KING'

This variegated holly is a radiant addition to the winter garden. To guarantee its glossy berries, you'll need to plant a male nearby. **H19ft (6m)**

OTHERS TO TRY

- *Bergenia* 'Sunningdale'
- *Chamaecyparis* 'Nana Gracilis'
- *Clematis cirrhosa* var *balearica*
- *Clematis urophylla* 'Winter Beauty'
- *Cornus alba* 'Sibirica'
- *Cyclamen coum*
- *Picea glauca* 'J.W. Daisy's White'
- *Hippeastrum* 'Papillo' (indoors)
- *Lonicera x purpusii* 'Winter Beauty'
- *Sarcococca confusa*

DECEMBER 2014

MONDAY
1

TUESDAY
2

WEDNESDAY
3

THURSDAY
4

FRIDAY
5

SATURDAY
6

SUNDAY
7

MONDAY
8

AT A GLANCE
JOBS TO DO THIS MONTH

GENERAL TASKS

- ☐ Put salt on icy paths but keep it away from nearby plants.
- ☐ Clean fallen leaves from gutters.
- ☐ Order seed catalogues.

LAWNS

- ☐ Don't walk on lawns if it's frosty as you'll kill the grass.
- ☐ Rake up any fallen leaves – lack of light will cause the lawn to die off.

TREES, SHRUBS AND CLIMBERS

- ☐ Only plant if the soil isn't frozen.
- ☐ Check newly planted trees haven't been lifted by the frost.
- ☐ Protect newly planted evergreens with a windbreak made from posts and fleece, rather like a beach windbreak.
- ☐ Choose your Christmas tree: Norway spruce is traditional but Nordmann Fir has better needle retention.

Saw an inch or so off the bottom of Christmas tree trunks to enable them to absorb more water

DECEMBER 2014

TUESDAY
9

WEDNESDAY
10

THURSDAY
11

FRIDAY
12

SATURDAY
13

SUNDAY
14

MONDAY
15

TUESDAY
16

Keep topping up bird feeders

Your notes

WEATHER:

PLANTS IN BLOOM:

TO DO:

DECEMBER 2014

WEDNESDAY
17

THURSDAY
18

FRIDAY
19

SATURDAY
20

SUNDAY
21

MONDAY
22

TUESDAY
23

WEDNESDAY
24

AT A GLANCE
JOBS TO DO THIS MONTH

FLOWERS

- ☐ Protect herbaceous plants vulnerable to frost, like penstemons, by covering the crowns with a layer of bracken or straw.
- ☐ Continue to cut down perennials, weed and tidy borders when the weather permits.
- ☐ Continue to clear fallen leaves from the crowns of alpines and rock gardens.
- ☐ Sow alpine seeds and leave pots outside, with a sheet of glass over the top to protect from the wet – the cold will break seed dormancy.

IN THE GREENHOUSE

- ☐ Check bulbs, corms and tubers in store.
- ☐ Bring forced bulbs indoors into the warmth and light.
- ☐ Pot up lilies for flowers in the spring.
- ☐ Check that greenhouse heaters are still working; adjust thermostat if needed.
- ☐ Reduce watering to a minimum.
- ☐ Bring bay trees undercover to protect them from the cold.

WHAT TO PRUNE

- **Renovate deciduous shrubs like forsythia and philadelphus**
- **Prune deciduous trees and shrubs for health and shape**

DECEMBER 2014

THURSDAY
25

FRIDAY
26

SATURDAY
27

SUNDAY
28

MONDAY
29

TUESDAY
30

WEDNESDAY
31

Check that greenhouse heaters are still working

Your notes

WEATHER:

PLANTS IN BLOOM:

TO DO:

Prune apple and pear trees

Winter pruning of apple and pear trees is needed to control their shape and size, encourage flowers and fruit, and to improve the overall health of the trees. This only applies to non-trained trees – cordons, espaliers and stepover trees can be left alone now, and instead be given a light trim in the summer.

Apple and pear trees are either spur or tip-bearing, and how you prune will vary slightly depending on which type you have. Pruning should be carried out on a dry day between late November and late February, after leaf fall and before bud burst.

Don't prune stone fruits (peaches, plums or cherries) at this time as you would make them susceptible to silver leaf disease, the spores of which are active at this time of year and can easily enter the pruning wounds.

TOP TIP

Keep secateurs and loppers sharp so they cut cleanly through wood; ragged cuts made with blunt tools can invite disease to enter trees

SPUR BEARERS

Most apple and pear trees are spur-bearing. Fruit is produced on short knobbly side growth (spurs) along the branch length. Encourage new spurs by pruning a sideshoot back to four or five buds from its base. The following winter look for buds on the same sideshoot that are fatter and more rounded than the pointy buds above – cut back to these to form fruiting spurs.

TIP BEARERS

Some varieties, such as 'Bramley's Seedling' and 'Blenheim Orange' are tip-bearers, which means that they produce the fruit buds on the tips of the previous year's shoots, instead of on short knobbly side growth (spurs). Shoot tips should be left unpruned, unless they are vigorous and more than a foot long. Prune back some older fruited wood to a new shoot, to reduce congestion.

WHAT TO AIM FOR

The aim of winter pruning of apples and pears is to remove congested branches to allow light to reach the centre of the plant, so that the fruit will mature well. New spurs should be encouraged by pruning side branches back, and new growth on the main branches should be cut by about a third to encourage the development of new branches.

Step by step How to prune apple trees

1 Prune out dead, diseased or damaged branches; ensure you cut right back into healthy wood.

2 Next, take out old, unproductive branches. This will usually be thicker wood so use loppers.

3 Spurs can become congested. Remove the oldest spurs to allow the younger ones to thrive.

4 Shorten young sideshoots to about five buds to stimulate new spur production at the base.

December

THE EDIBLE GARDEN - OTHER JOBS TO DO THIS MONTH

PLANT

- Fruit trees and bushes – if the soil isn't frozen or too wet

HARVEST

- Continue to harvest winter crops, such as leeks and parsnips that are being stored in the ground

PRUNE

- Gooseberry bushes now to retain an open-centred shape
- Grapevines

GENERAL TASKS

- **Remove lower** leaves of Brussels sprouts as they die
- **Check over** stored fruit: remove rotten ones
- **Continue to plan** the vegetable garden
- **Avoid walking** on bare soil when it's wet, as you'll cause compaction
- **Earth up** Brussels sprouts and other brassicas to prevent wind damage
- **Take hardwood cuttings** of currants and gooseberries

December project

Grow Christmas roses

DESPITE ITS rather enticing common name, the Christmas rose (*Helleborus niger*) is not really a rose at all and is rarely in flower at Christmas time.

It got its nickname because the pure-white saucers studded with golden-yellow anthers were thought to resemble wild roses, but in fact, the Christmas rose is an early-flowering hellebore, appearing a good few weeks before its more commonly grown cousin, *Helleborus orientalis*.

In gardens, its beautiful virginal white flowers usually appear in January and February, but it's possible to force them into flower for Christmas, by growing them in containers.

TOP TIP

Christmas roses make good houseplants, flowering until spring, but should be moved or planted outdoors thereafter

The Christmas rose thrives in soil that's rich and fertile but on the alkaline side. It also prefers its crown kept dry, a deep root run and a sunny spot to bring out the flowers – all the more reasons to grow it in a pot, where you can control the growing conditions.

Containers should be kept relatively cool and shaded over summer, but can be moved into the greenhouse or a sheltered spot in late autumn, so that the plants bud up and flower in time for Christmas.

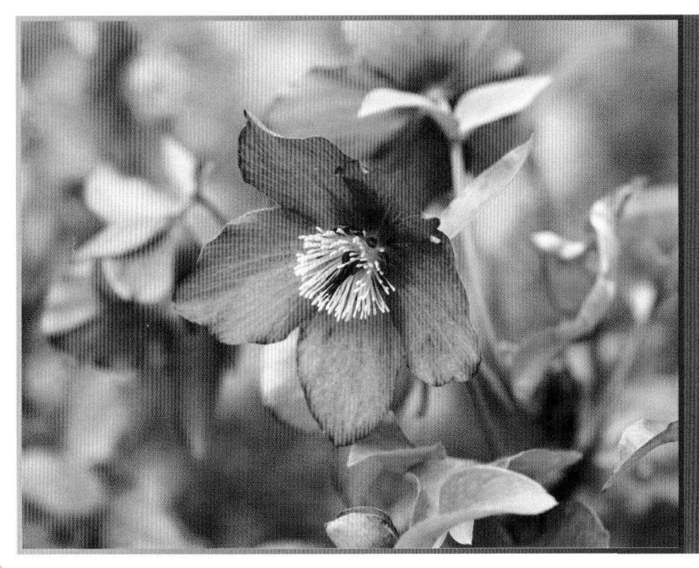

BEST VARIETIES

- **'Walberton's Rosemary'** (pictured) Lovely pink flowers.
- **Harvington double white** Gorgeous double blooms.
- **'Potter's Wheel'** Very floriferous, with round, pure-white flowers.
- **Ashwood Strain** Well formed, cup-shaped flowers of purest white on strong stems.

HOW TO GROW IN POTS

■ **Start off by buying cheaper 'tester' *Helleborus niger* in smaller pots for around £3. If possible, buy them in flower, looking for rounded blooms and plenty of healthy foliage. Then, if you have success, progress to more sought-after (and pricier) varieties.**

■ Pot them into slightly larger containers – either singly in individual pots or two or three together in a larger container. It's important to use a free-draining, soil-based compost such as John Innes No3. Place against a warm wall.

■ **Once they've finished flowering move into a dryish position in semi-shade, but continue watering once a week so that good-looking foliage is produced. Deadhead the flowers.**

■ Repot your hellebores into slightly larger pots every year during the second half of summer. When repotting add some slow-release fertiliser – hellebores are hungry plants. Move them back to the warm wall in late autumn.

■ **If you need to divide plants after a few years, split into two or three large pieces, but generally it's best to leave well alone.**

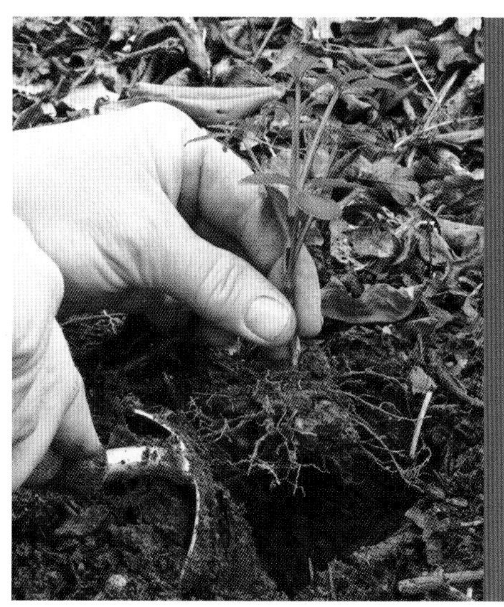

PROPAGATION

Raising your own hellebores from seed is a good way to get extra plants – although only species will come true to type. Hellebores set lots of large seeds that ripen in May or June. Sow these straightaway whilst ripe. Gently push them into pots of seed compost. Cover with a shallow layer of grit, then water lightly. Leave outside in partial shade over winter and seedlings will start to appear in February/March. Alternatively, let mother nature take her course and wait for seedlings to appear in the ground. Simply dig these up and transplant them where you want (pictured).